SpringerBriefs in Arts-Based Educational Research

Series Editor

Mindy Carter, Department of Integrated Studies in Education, McGill University, Montréal, QC, Canada

Editorial Board

Pam Burnard, University of Cambridge, Cambridge, UK

Qiana Cutts, Mississippi State University, Mississippi, MS, USA

Walter S. Gershon, School of Teaching Learning, Kent State University, Kent, OH, USA

Peter Gouzouasis, The University of British Columbia, Vancouver, BC, Canada

Andrea Kantrowitz, State University of New York, Pelham, NY, USA

Kelly Clark/Keefe, College of Education and Social Services, University of Vermont, Burlington, VT, USA

Diane Kuthy, Towson University, Towson, MD, USA

Morna McDermott McNulty, Towson University, Towson, MD, USA

Layal Shuman, Toronto Metropolitan University, Toronto, ON, Canada

Richard Siegesmund, School of Art and Design, Northern Illinois University, Dekalb, IL, USA

Arts-Based Educational Research continues to garner increased interest and debate among artists, arts writers, researchers, scholars and educators internationally. Further, the methodologies and theoretical articulations associated with Arts-Based Educational Research are increasingly employed across the disciplines of social science, education, humanities, health, media, communication, the creative arts, design, and transdisciplinary and interdisciplinary research.

This book series offers edited collections and monographs that survey and exemplify Arts-Based Educational Research. The series will take up questions relevant to the diverse range of Arts-Based Educational Research. These questions might include: What can Arts-Based methodologies (such as Arts-Based Research, Arts-Informed Research, a/r/tography, Poetic Inquiry, Performative Inquiry, Arts Practice-Based Research etc.) do as a form of critical qualitative inquiry? How do the Arts (such as literary, visual and performing arts) enable research? What is the purpose of Arts-Based Educational Research? What counts as Arts-Based? What counts as Educational? What counts as Research? How can Arts-Based Educational Research be responsibly performed in communities and institutions, individually or collaboratively? Must Arts-Based Educational Research be public? What ways of knowing and being can be explored with Arts-Based Educational Research? How can Arts-Based Educational Research build upon diverse philosophical, theoretical, historical, political, aesthetic and spiritual approaches to living? What is not Arts-Based Educational Research?

The hinge connecting the arts and research in this Arts-Based Educational Research book series is education. Education is understood in its broadest sense as learning/transformation/change that takes place in diverse formal and informal spaces, places and moments. As such, books in this series might take up questions such as: How do perspectives on education, curriculum and pedagogy (such as critical, participatory, liberatory, intercultural and historical) inform Arts-Based inquiries? How do teachers become artists, and how do artists become teachers? How can one be both? What does this look like, in and beyond school environments?

The book series also addresses critical questions at the intersections across the arts and education. The possible expressions of this intersection is broadly defined with particular interest in works that attend to and otherwise center constructions of Indigeneity, race, gender, gender identity and expression, sexual orientation, nationality, movement and migration, neurodiversity, and the like. The volumes in the series take on topics, in multiple ways, including: pushing at false boundaries between disciplinary silos; theoretical foundations from questions including those regarding might be considered arts and education; and modes of expression and method/ologies that press at current constructions. In keeping with these commitments, the series continues to explicitly broaden the diversity of its editorial board in both identity and focus of research.

Arts-Based Educational Research will be deeply and broadly explored, represented, questioned and developed in this vital and digitally augmented international publication series. The aesthetic reach of this series will be expanded by a digital online repository where all media pertaining to publications will be held. Queries can be sent via email to Mindy Carter editor.aber.springer@gmail.com.

Marcy Meyer

Iconographic Research Poetry

Marcy Meyer
Department of Communication Studies
Ball State University
Muncie, Indiana, USA

ISSN 2524-7506   ISSN 2524-7514 (electronic)
SpringerBriefs in Arts-Based Educational Research
ISBN 978-981-97-2374-4   ISBN 978-981-97-2375-1 (eBook)
https://doi.org/10.1007/978-981-97-2375-1

© The Author(s) 2024. This book is an open access publication.

Open Access This book is licensed under the terms of the Creative Commons Attribution 4.0 International License (http://creativecommons.org/licenses/by/4.0/), which permits use, sharing, adaptation, distribution and reproduction in any medium or format, as long as you give appropriate credit to the original author(s) and the source, provide a link to the Creative Commons license and indicate if changes were made.

The images or other third party material in this book are included in the book's Creative Commons license, unless indicated otherwise in a credit line to the material. If material is not included in the book's Creative Commons license and your intended use is not permitted by statutory regulation or exceeds the permitted use, you will need to obtain permission directly from the copyright holder.

The use of general descriptive names, registered names, trademarks, service marks, etc. in this publication does not imply, even in the absence of a specific statement, that such names are exempt from the relevant protective laws and regulations and therefore free for general use.

The publisher, the authors and the editors are safe to assume that the advice and information in this book are believed to be true and accurate at the date of publication. Neither the publisher nor the authors or the editors give a warranty, expressed or implied, with respect to the material contained herein or for any errors or omissions that may have been made. The publisher remains neutral with regard to jurisdictional claims in published maps and institutional affiliations.

This Springer imprint is published by the registered company Springer Nature Singapore Pte Ltd.
The registered company address is: 152 Beach Road, #21-01/04 Gateway East, Singapore 189721, Singapore

If disposing of this product, please recycle the paper.

In loving memory of my father, Arthur Miller Covell, who sends me free verse from beyond.

Foreword—An Interruption to the Straight Line

Growing up in Te Tai Tokerau, the North of the North Island of New Zealand, we all knew the resident Austrian architect and artist Friedensreich Hundertwasser. We knew him, perhaps not by his name as much as by the public toilets he sculpted in the main street of the small town of Kawakawa. The eccentric design comprising juxtaposed tiles, curvaceous ceramics, colored glass, with a roof of living grasses, soon became an international tourist attraction. Unlike any other building on the main street, the restrooms were alive because of the sculpture's nonlinearity. I found it unsurprising to learn, then, that Hundertwasser (1985) once declared "the straight line leads to the downfall of [hu]mankind" (para. 7). He contended that the straight line is allied to "rationalist knowhow" (para. 9) and ultimately leads to the loss of creative power. As for visual art, so may be the case for poetry. It may be common sense that we imagine ourselves speaking in lines. We have given language its marching orders, parading from out of us, and before us, in prosaic rank and file. Yet, what Meyer's *Iconographic Research Poetry* gives us is an interruption to the straight line.

Meyer names for us a new form of research poetry: iconographic research poetry, based upon the literary heritage of concrete and visual poets. Meyer traces its research lineage to poetic inquiry, within arts-based research. On one hand, this book shares the personal story of Meyer's own journey from a quantitative researcher to an arts-based researcher; as Meyer relays, this process was about freeing her creativity. Her journey reflects the wrestling for authentic representation in research, characteristic of her earlier autoethnographic study focusing on the experiences of caregivers of children with mental illnesses. At this point, I discern Meyer consciously departed from the traditional research line. Perhaps because of those deeply personal connections to participants we hold alongside the responsibility of ethical representation, we are called upon to break the line. For Meyer, this has resulted in migrating language to visualized shapes, giving

language a	fresh
embodiment,	a new way of
speaking in	and of the world.
Meyer has	created a window

in research from which one can see constellations, crows, and the Virgin of Guadalupe. On the other hand, this book is an arts-based research master class. It gets us up to speed with the full conceptual framework for undertaking arts-based research. In a pedagogical sense, Meyer does not leave us with a theoretical discussion; instead, she provides us with practical advice for getting to work on our own iconographic research study and teaching. Meyer gives guidance on how we can "fill up our inner well of creativity," and how to translate artistic nuance to the page: "Using the tab key, space bar, and hard returns, create the shape of a mountain."

I conclude with a spoiler alert. You will hear Meyer comment that the early concrete and visual poets considered their artwork a universal language. This observation holds promise for this fledgling arts-based research practice. Iconographic research poetry opens the possibility for intercultural communication in a world that seems increasingly divided on lines of nationality, politics, religion, ethnicity, gender and sexuality, socio-economic status, and disability/ableism. What if iconographic research poets were to call out the divides? What if iconographic research poets could bridge those divides with empathy and compassion? What if iconographic research poets could perform new ways of dwelling together in harmony? What if iconographic research poetry could change the world? I think this is wholly possible if we take the courage, as Meyer has, to begin with a break to the straight line.

Adrian Schoone, Ph.D.
Auckland University of Technology
Auckland, New Zealand

Reference

Hundertwasser, F. (1985). Hundertwasser. *The paradise destroyed by the straight line.* https://www.hundertwasser.com/en/texts/ueber_das_durch_die_gerade_linie_zerstoerte_paradies

Series Editor's Foreword

Will You, Won't You, Join in Writing Research Poetry?

My interest in poetry as research writing and poetic inquiry was ignited by Carl Leggo in the early 1990s. Through his works, and the writings of very talented graduate students—namely Rishma Dunlop and Karen V. Lee—who were drawn to Carl and his role in the emerging realm of Arts-Based Educational Research (ABER), I dove into a new wonderland.

Hand searching through journals, I unearthed the names of those whose root works became part of my vernacular by the turn of the new millennium—Eisner, Barone, Clandinin, Connelly, Donmoyer, Paley, Van Maanen, van Manen, Aoki, Ellis, Furman, Glesne, Carr, Luce-Kapler, MacNeill, Neilsen, Richardson, Sparkes, and many others. The offshoots of those underground channels led me into deeper dives of many journals that were far removed from music and music research. However, that was my learning pathway through the rhizomatically connected, exploratory, networked growth into autoethnography and ABR. Over two decades later, insightful researchers such as Marcy Meyer—the author of the current monograph—have realized what were once merely potential connections between the humanities, creative social science, and arts-based research.

From my perspective, the connective rhizomes of many talented, creative researcher-writers have bloomed to fruition in the hands of *artistresearcherteachers*[1] the past two decades and they are revealed in this lush, magnificent book.

While I am not a poet in the strict sense of the craft,[2] I've been a singer-songwriter since the late 1960s. As a young boy, I was drawn to the elegantly crafted, poetic

---

[1] See Gouzouasis (2008) for a rationale on the removal of slashes that signify the "a/r/t" of artography.

[2] See Gouzouasis & Leggo (2016) and Gouzouasis (2018). I'd be remiss not to mention Monica Prendergast who was a post-doctoral candidate who worked with the a/r/tography group (Peter Gouzouasis, Kit Grauer, Rita Irwin, & Carl Leggo) at the University of British Columbia and contributed to the creation of a landmark, poetic inquiry paper in music research (see Prendergast et al., 2009).

lyrics of many musicians—from Carole King, Joni Mitchell, Laura Nyro, Janis Ian, Carley Simon, and Bonnie Raitt to Bob Dylan, Paul Simon, Kris Kristofferson, John Prine, Gordon Lightfoot, James Taylor, and Jimmy Webb, to the songwriting teams of Felice and Boudleaux Bryant, Barry Mann and Cynthia Weill, Walter Becker and Donald Fagen, Elton John and Bernie Taupin, and John Lennon and Paul McCartney. Through them, running back and forth through subterranean-stemmed audio channels, I learned even more by listening to popular singers of the 1930s–1960s and the poetic lyrics of Cole Porter, Ira Gershwin, Harold Arlen, Lorenz Hart, Oscar Hammerstein, Betty Comden and Adolph Green, Johnny Burke, Tom Adair, Johnny Mercer, and Sammy Cahn. Collectively, all that music (in)formed the musical mosaic of an adolescent raised through the shifting carrier waves of amplitude modulation (AM) radio that led to the frequency modulation (FM) radio revolution of pop-folk-rock singer-songwriters.

Thus, when I think of the image—the *eikóna*—of poetry,[3] my ideas modulate to rhythmic and melodic patterns, tempos, dynamics, articulations, and other musical features that can be metaphorically and metonymically used to shape words and ultimately, the expressivity that words may evoke through poetic forms and song. Like rich soil, sunlight, and water, those kinds of enriching ideas have cultivated my interest in teaching at least one unit of poetic inquiry in autoethnography and arts-based research courses at UBC over the past two decades. And they once inspired me to compose a poem for an early a/r/tographic exploration in tonality.[4]

---

[3] As a Greek speaker, I am informed by the spelling of "image" as *eikóna* (from the Greek, εικόνα, where 'ei' sounds as the diphthong, 'ee').

[4] Gouzouasis (2007, p. 42) was written in Winter 2002–2003 for the first a/r/tography book; however, it became evident that *a/r/tography: Rendering self through arts-based living inquiry* (Irwin & de Cosson, 2004) was intended for a visual artist audience. Though obliterated by the journal editors, as well as omitting a full structural and harmonic analysis of the first movement of Beethoven's Piano Sonata (opus 109) that inspired the overall form of the eventually published article, the textual shape of the poem was originally meant to evoke the image of an upright bass. I didn't know how to explain it or what to call it in 2007. That is yet another reason why Marcy Meyer's book is long overdue.

Series Editor's Foreword

<pre>
              still   string
              dead   wood
              mindful music
              thoughts speak

                through
                 each
                finger
                  a
                voice
                 that
                sounds
                ideas
                from
                 the
               passages
                  of
                  my
                 soul
            DYNAMIC variations
             timbreal rainbows
            art ic u la tions abound
             I pluck my heartstrings
             t h i n k i n g
              feeling vibrations

               I breathe life
               into my guitar
               a genesis of

                 music
                  and
                 truth
</pre>

© Peter Gouzouasis

Marcy Meyer's ideas are robust and inspirational. They inspirit us to live poetically, to live musically, and to live artfully. Her approach to teaching and learning iconographic research poetry is clear, creative, and cohesive. Most importantly, her playful approach is accessible and applicable across any discipline. Marcy's exhilarating ideas have led me through even more fertile learning pathways that will surely nourish people who read this enthralling book. I've already shared it with close colleagues, and I will use it in the next ABER-autoethnography course I teach, as soon as it's released in the *Springer ABER Series*.

To play with the Mock Turtle's song, I call you to dance into the artful action of iconographic poetry. With Marcy Meyer's perceptive creative direction, you can joyously join in writing iconographic poetry.

Peter Gouzouasis, Ph.D. (Music)
Professor
The University of British Columbia
Vancouver, Canada

References

Gouzouasis, P. (2007). Music research in an a/r/tographic tonality. *Journal of the Canadian Association for Curriculum Studies, 5*(2), 33–58.

Gouzouasis, P. (2008). Toccata on assessment, validity, and interpretation. In S. Springgay, R. L. Irwin, P. Gouzouasis, & C. Leggo (Eds.), *Being with a/r/t/ography* (pp. 219–230). Sense Publishers.

Gouzouasis, P. & Leggo, C. (2016). Performative research in music and poetry: A pedagogy of listening. In P. Burnard, L. Mackinlay, & K. Powell (Eds.), *The Routledge international handbook of intercultural arts research* (pp. 454–466). Taylor & Francis/Routledge.

Gouzouasis, P. (2018). A/r/tographic inquiry in a new tonality: The relationality of music and poetry. In P. Leavy (Ed.), *Handbook of arts based research* (pp. 233–246). Guilford Press.

Prendergast, M., Gouzouasis, P., Leggo, C., & Irwin, R. (2009). A haiku suite: The importance of music making in the lives of secondary students. *Music Education Research, 11*(3), 303–317.

Preface

Have you ever fallen asleep reading a research methods text before? I have, and let me tell you, it's dangerous. Because they're heavy and have hard covers and sharp corners, you can literally lose an eye if you attempt to read them while propped up in bed. At the end of a long day, when you can no longer keep your eyes open and your head starts nodding, the slick book slips out of your hands. When you jerk awake, the book boomerangs and one sharp corner nearly detaches your retina. That's why I wear glasses when I read in bed. And prefer my books in soft cover.

In case you haven't already guessed, this book is going to be different than other research methods texts that you have read. Prepare yourself, because it may violate your expectations (in a good way, I hope). I'd like to begin this book by getting acquainted. Let's start with you. Who are you? How are you feeling today? Why are you reading this book? I hope you're not reading in bed at night. I hope that it's morning and you're well rested and you're reading in a comfortable chair with a good cup of coffee or tea. I hope you are feeling happy and healthy and curious about what today will bring. Wherever you are, take a minute and check in with yourself.

Next, I'd like to introduce myself to you. I am a middle-aged, highly educated, middle-class, divorced European American woman and single mother. Autoimmune diseases and mental illness run in my family. I am the youngest of seven children and a third-generation teacher. I grew up in rural New Hampshire, then attended Georgetown University, in Washington, DC, where I studied international relations. I spent my junior year studying abroad in Fribourg, Switzerland, where I lived with a Suisse Romande family and took university classes in French. After I earned my bachelor's degree, I pursued dual masters' degrees in communication and urban studies at Michigan State University. It was there that I earned my Ph.D. in communication, which made me the first person in my family to earn a doctorate. I am proud of my achievement, as well as the fact that my dissertation won the W. Charles Redding Award, which recognizes the year's outstanding dissertation in organizational communication. However, I would be remiss if I failed to mention that I am neither the most intelligent person in my family nor the author of the best organizational communication dissertation in my cohort. I realize that my accomplishments are due in large part to my privileged social position as a White middle-class person raised by educators. Without the support and encouragement of my family and mentors, I would not be who I am today.

Full disclosure: The year that I graduated from Ph.D. school, I learned to ride a bicycle. Although I had written an award-winning dissertation, I was—and still am—a novice in many areas of my life. When I was trained as a logical empiricist and quantitative methodologist in graduate school, I felt like I had to lock my creativity away in a time capsule. Soon after I took my first job at Ball State University, I began the process of freeing my creative inner child. Thanks to supportive university, college, and departmental cultures that valued innovation and academic freedom, I was able to experiment with diverse methodological approaches. First, I reinvented myself as a qualitative scholar by collaborating on a research project with Laura O'Hara, a colleague trained as an ethnographer who generously shared her knowledge with me. Next, I learned how to conduct autoethnographic research, mentored by Angie Day, a junior colleague who was well versed in creative approaches to research. While I was studying autoethnography, I became interested in research poetry. I started out writing autoethnographic free verse poetry. Inspired by Laura Ellingson's work on crystallization, I became fascinated by alternative modes of representation. While experimenting with different forms of poetic inquiry, I invented a new form of research poetry: iconographic research poetry. My desire to share this alternative form of representation with others set me on the path that led me to write this book.

Back to you. You may be wondering whether or not this book is for you. Maybe you have been taught to believe that research should be empirical, objective, and unbiased. You ask yourself, "Why should I read a book about iconographic research poetry?" Good question. Why should you? I know we're only on page xiv, but I would like you to stop reading now. Please take out a notebook and pen or open a word processing program on your laptop. Write down three reasons why you should keep reading. There's no right or wrong answer to this question. Just write.

Okay. Are you done? Great! There are a couple of reasons why I asked you to consider why you want to read this book. The first is because of some wise advice that I learned from Jeff Davis, a creative writing instructor who practices yoga poetry. He wrote, "Yoga without intention is just exercise." The same is true for reading. If you have a clear intention for reading this book, whether it be to learn something new, to exercise your creativity, or to help yourself fall asleep at night, you will get more out of what you read. The next reason I asked you why you want to read this book was a pretext to get you to start writing. If you're not already in the habit of writing every day, then you just did something very important. Without exception, all of the good writers that I know make writing a daily practice. If you haven't already begun this practice, you should congratulate yourself for starting today.

Finally, in asking you why you want to read this book, I want to challenge you to think critically about what constitutes valid research. You may have had research methods teachers in the past who taught you that science should be logical, rational, empirical, and unbiased. Although those characteristics may describe some types of traditional quantitative social science research, they do not pertain to all types of research. Indeed, I have learned that it is not possible to conduct unbiased research because all humans are innately biased—instead, it is important for researchers to be aware of and open about their biases. In other words, reflexivity is an essential characteristic of research. In addition to testing hypotheses and constructing logical arguments supported by data, research can also evoke emotion, build interpersonal relationships, and pose questions that foster curiosity and creativity.

In 30 years of studying and conducting research, I have moved across the continuum, from a traditional quantitative researcher to a creative qualitative researcher and iconographic research poet. Although I won an international award for my (quantitative) dissertation, I also have faced colleagues and respondents who dismissed and invalidated my autoethnographic research, questioning the legitimacy of my work and refusing to respond to autoethnographic papers that I wrote under a pen name in order to protect the identities of my family members. Having experienced both the privilege of international acclaim from those who laud quantitative research and the prejudice of those who do not understand or accept creative qualitative research, I feel compelled to share my perspective with you. I hope that you will feel supported and encouraged to produce your own creative work, as well as to educate others who may be ignorant about alternative forms of research. Please remain curious. No matter what the grown-ups say, do not lock your creative inner child away in a time capsule.

Muncie, Indiana, USA   Marcy Meyer

Acknowledgements

This book was funded in part by a special assigned leave from Ball State University. Thanks to my provosts, deans, chairs, staff, and colleagues in the Department of Communication Studies who supported me and encouraged me to write this book.

I will be forever grateful to Angie Day and Laura Ellingson, who mentored me with such kindness and intellectual generosity at the beginning of my creative qualitative journey.

Heartfelt thanks to my friends in NAMI and 401 Poetry, who provided me with inspiration for my initial foray into iconographic research poetry.

I am grateful to so many people for supporting this project.

First, thanks to the Springer editorial and production teams, who provided me w/ affirmation and support throughout the review and production processes.

Special thanks to Kaitlyn Helmer, who contributed to the section on graphic design, and Jenna Cantrell, who taught me how to convert my old-school MS Word clip art into state-of-the-art 21st c. digital images.

I am grateful to the members of the International Symposium on Poetic Inquiry for creating and nurturing a community in which poetic inquiry can thrive.

Artful thanks to Gordon Coons and Ann & Christa Barnell, whose beautiful, brilliant paintings sparked iconographic ekphrastic poetry.

I am indebted to the Estate of Mary Ellen Solt for giving me permission to reprint "Forsythia."

Last but not least, I would like to express my undying gratitude to my family and friends for their love & support. *Without roots, a tree is*

Thanks also to my students, who motivated me to think of innovative ways to integrate ABR within the creative culture classroom.

just a log. Thank you for keeping me rooted, so I could branch out and leaf in my creative dream, spilling words in constellations across the sky.

Contents

1   **Introduction** 1
    1.1   Key Concepts 2
    1.2   History 5
    1.3   Summary 14
    1.4   Why Iconographic Research Poetry? 14
    1.5   Preview of the Book 15
    References 17

2   **Methods: Designing Iconographic Research Poetry** 23
    2.1   The Qualitative Continuum 24
    2.2   Analysis 25
    2.3   Representation 27
    2.4   Member and Artist-Poet Reflections 33
    2.5   Summary 34
    2.6   Exercises 35
    References 36

3   **The State of Concrete and Iconographic Research Poetry** 39
    3.1   From Casserole to Constellation: A Review of Concrete
         and Iconographic Research Poetry 40
    3.2   Iconographic Ekphrastic Poetic Inquiry 45
    3.3   Reflexive Analysis 52
    3.4   Exercises 55
    References 56

4   **Iconographic Research Poetry in the Classroom** 59
    4.1   Arts-Based Research Pedagogy 60
    4.2   Pedagogical Innovations 61
    4.3   Debriefing 64
    References 65

5 Conclusion and New Beginnings 67
  5.1 Summary 68
  5.2 Strengths and Limitations 69
  5.3 Directions for Future Research 71
  5.4 Poetic Inquiry as a Transformational Practice 72
  5.5 Additional Resources 72
  References 74

6 Postscript 77
  6.1 Living Poetically in Community 80
  References 81

Index 83

About the Author

Marcy Meyer (BS, Georgetown University; MA, PhD, Michigan State University) is an Associate Professor in the Department of Communication Studies at Ball State University and an Associate Editor at *Art/Research International: A Transdisciplinary Journal*. A winner of the 1996 ICA Redding Dissertation Award and the 2001 CSCA Federation Prize, Marcy has presented and published her research about organizational communication, innovation, mentoring, diversity, & research poetry internationally. Marcy lives in Muncie, IN, USA, on land that was cared for by the Myaamia (Miami) and Lenape (Delaware).

Chapter 1
Introduction

Abstract In this chapter, the author identifies, defines, and illustrates the book's key concepts, including concrete poetry, iconographic poetry, research poetry, poetic inquiry, and iconographic research poetry. Next, the author offers brief overviews of the history of concrete poetry, iconographic poetry, poetic inquiry, and research poetry, four central areas of inquiry that have inspired the notion of iconographic research poetry. The author explores the intellectual foundations that undergird the concept of iconographic research poetry by reviewing classic and contemporary texts from the humanities and social sciences. After enumerating the advantages of iconographic research poetry and positioning it as a methodological innovation that bridges art, literature, and science, the author concludes this chapter with a preview of the book.

Keywords Arts-based research (ABR) · Arts-based educational research (ABER) · ABR methods · Concrete poetry · Iconographic poetry · Iconographic research poetry · Poetic inquiry · Research poetry

The central goal of this book is to offer readers an introduction to the craft of writing *iconographic research poetry*. Previously referred to as concrete research poetry (Meyer, 2017), iconographic research poetry is a novel form of poetic inquiry that bridges the art-science divide by melding aspects of iconographic poetry and research poetry. By tracing the historical foundations of concrete and iconographic research poetry, as well as the development of research poetry and poetic inquiry, I hope to offer the reader an appreciation for the intellectual roots that inform this unique methodological approach. In the process, I invite previously unrelated areas of inquiry into dialogue with one another.

I begin this chapter by defining key concepts such as concrete poetry, iconographic poetry, research poetry, poetic inquiry, and iconographic research poetry. I offer exemplars to illustrate each type of poetry that I introduce. Next, I provide brief overviews of the history of concrete poetry, iconographic poetry, poetic inquiry, and research poetry, four central areas of inquiry that have inspired the notion of iconographic research poetry. Drawing on classic and contemporary texts from the humanities and social sciences (e.g., Bean & McCabe, 2015; Bohn, 2011; Butler-Kisber, 2002; Faulkner, 2009, 2020; Funkhouser, 2007; Goldsmith, 2009; Hill & Vassilakis, 2012; Hollander, 1975; Kostelanetz, 1970; Lahman, 2022; Leavy, 2009, 2015, 2020; Solt, 1968; Swenson, 1970), I trace the intellectual foundations that undergird the concept of iconographic research poetry. Next, I consider the advantages of iconographic research poetry as a methodological innovation that bridges the humanities and the social sciences. I conclude this chapter with a preview of the book.

1.1 Key Concepts

Concrete poetry has been conceptualized in many different ways. Kostelanetz (1970) defined concrete poetry as "word-imagery," or "artifacts that are neither word nor image alone but somewhere or something between" para. (1). Kostelanetz identified two types of word-imagery: imaged words and worded images. Imaged words, which may consist of one word or one word repeated in a pattern are perhaps more closely related to art than to poetry. One classic example of an imaged word is Robert Indiana's 1970 sculpture "LOVE." This iconic work of pop art has been reproduced around the world in many different colors and languages. Pictured here is the LOVE sculpture in New Castle, Indiana, Robert Indiana's hometown. (See Fig. 1.1.)

Kostelanetz's (1970) second type of concrete poem is the worded image. This vision of concrete poetry is congruent with Solt's description of a concrete poem as an "ideogram or a constellation" of words (Solt, 1968, p. 59). In this type of concrete poem, the "language fills an image, embellishing the shape through linguistic means... making pictures with words and letters" (Kostelanetz, 1970, para. 1). One brilliant example of a worded image is Mary Ellen Solt's "Forsythia," which employs the letters F-O-R-S-Y-T-H-I-A, in concert with their Morse Code equivalents, to form the roots and branches of a flowering shrub. (See Fig. 1.2.) This poem is a visual feast, as well as a puzzle to solve.

Closely related to Solt's concept of concrete poetry is May Swenson's *iconographic poetry*. Swenson (1970) derived the term "iconograph" from the Greek "eikonos," meaning "image" or "likeness" and "graphe," which means "carve" (p. 86). Similar to pattern poetry or shaped poetry (Hollander, 1967), an iconograph is an emblematic poem "in which the words or letters form a typographical picture" (Drury, 1995). Put differently, iconographic poems provide the reader with a text to read, as well as a visual object to perceive. By creating a gestalt visual image for the reader to decode, the poet preempts the linear, logical, sequential means by which humans typically process written communication word-by-word, line-by-line, paragraph-by-paragraph, and page-by-page. As the poem's physical form shapes the reader's interpretation, it interrupts the left brain's task of cognitive processing and invites the right brain to participate in the interpretive process, thereby creating space for a more emotionally evocative reading of the text.

1.1 Key Concepts

Fig. 1.1 Concrete poem (imaged word): LOVE sculpture in Arts Park, New Castle, Indiana (photograph). *Source* Bertram (2021). Used with permission

Perhaps because of its capacity for aesthetic, evocative representation, poetry has been embraced by art-based researchers, as well as literary scholars. Prendergast (2009) defined *poetic inquiry* as a "form of qualitative research in the social sciences that incorporates poetry in some way as a component of an investigation" (para. 1). Poetic inquirers may integrate poetry into a study's literature review, methods, analysis, or findings. Research poems differ from literary or creative poems in that they typically address issues related to conceptualization and methodology—in other words, research poetry should connect to existing scholarly literature and the methods should be shared for verification and replication (Lahman & Richard,

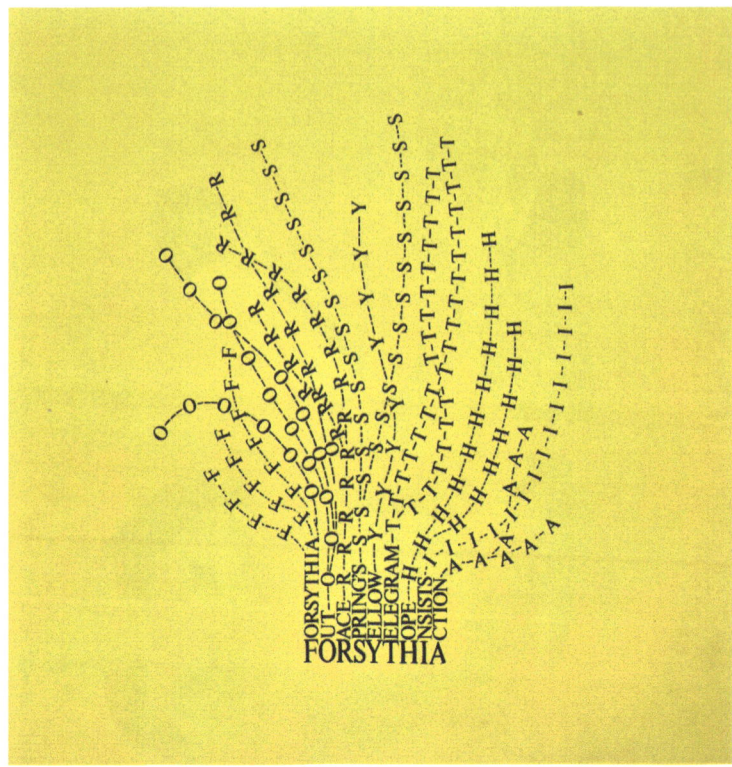

Fig. 1.2 Concrete poem (worded image): "Forsythia." *Source* Solt (1968). Reprinted by permission of the Estate of Mary Ellen Solt

2014). Sameshima et al. (2018) argued that poetic inquiry has profound epistemological and ontological implications for researchers, as it offers them an alternative way of knowing and conducting research, as well as "a way to be and become in the world" (Leggo, as cited in Sameshima et al., 2018, p. 16). In this sense, practicing poetic inquiry has the potential to change not only how scholars conduct research and represent their findings, but also who they are as human beings.

Research poetry (Faulkner, 2009) is a specific form of poetic inquiry in which scholars produce arts-based representations of research findings by creating poetry from qualitative data, such as interviews and observations (Leavy, 2015). Because most research poems transform existing text (e.g., interview transcripts) into poems (Lahman et al., 2011), they can be classified as found poetry (Butler-Kisber, 2002). Although some writers have intentionally contrasted multiple forms (e.g., Furman, 2006) or have experimented with specific forms such as haiku (e.g., Holman Jones, 2011; Lahman et al., 2011; Prendergast, 2004), most research poetry takes the form of free verse (e.g., Carr, 2003; Ellingson, 2011; Faulkner, 2005; Glesne, 1997). For example, Sjollema and Yuen (2017) wrote research poems that embodied their affective responses to interviews that they conducted with participants in an arts-based participatory action research project that sought to support and empower Indigenous women who were survivors of violent crime to become agents in their healing journeys. Sjollema wrote,

> I cried when you said
>
> you had a chance to feel proud
>
> came in touch
>
> with your own artist
>
> that the word "Aboriginal"
>
> means beauty
>
> means art (p. 117)

Sjollema and Yuen's research poetry offers a powerful affective representation of the research process—a confessional tale that would most likely not be told in a traditional methods section.

Iconographic research poetry melds the practices of iconographic poetry and research poetry in order to create poems that represent research findings in shapes that are symbolically significant. For example, in an autoethnographic study about the experiences of caregivers of children with mental illness (Meyer, 2017), I employed the shape of a rollercoaster to represent participants who compared their child's mood swings to a rollercoaster ride (See Fig. 1.3.) As I explain later in this chapter, iconographic research poetry has a number of distinct advantages because it offers the reader a visual shape that provides a cognitive schema for interpreting participants' words.

In sum, iconographic research poetry is a fusion of iconographic poetry and research poetry. On one hand is iconographic poetry. Akin to one type of concrete poetry, iconographic poems are shaped like the subject that the author is writing about. On the other hand is research poetry, a form of poetic inquiry in which scholars represent qualitative research findings via poetry. Figure 1.4 employs a Venn diagram to illustrate the relationships between concrete poetry, iconographic poetry, poetic inquiry, research poetry, and iconographic research poetry. Although these concepts are distinct, they also overlap to a certain extent. Iconographic research poetry is located at the nexus of these overlapping concepts.

1.2 History

Concrete and iconographic poetry. Literary scholars typically locate the roots of the concrete poetry movement in the 1950s with the Brazilian Noigandres group, an avant-garde group of writers, musicians, and artists; however, early examples of iconographic poetry may have existed as early as 300 B.C., when Greek poets such as Simmias of Rhodes created a series of shape poems (Hollander, 1975). Other

Fig. 1.3 Iconographic research poem: "Rollercoaster." *Source* Meyer (2017). Reprinted by permission of the author

It feels like

an

unending

roller

coaster:

I'm walking on eggshells, holding my breath

and

then

we

fall

into

the

abyss.

It isn't just waiting for the next shoe to fall—

It's

knowing

that

an

EXPLOSION

will

follow

the

shoe

that keeps me on edge.

1.2 History

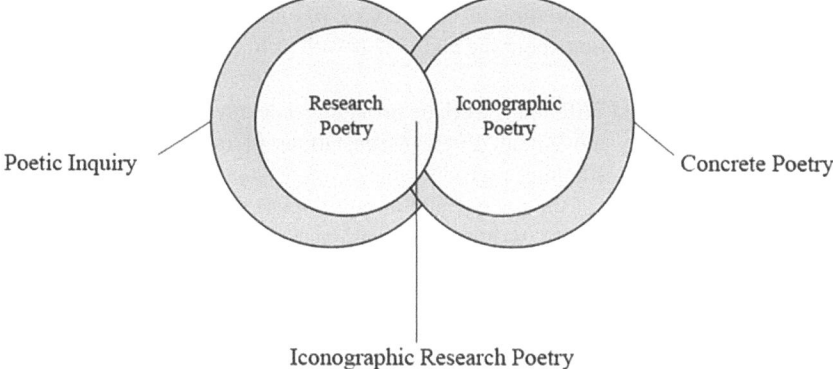

Fig. 1.4 Venn diagram of poetic inquiry, research poetry, concrete poetry, iconographic poetry, and iconographic research poetry

examples of iconographic poetry, such as George Herbert's "Easter Wings" (Herbert, 1633), Lewis Carroll's "Mouse's Tale" (Carroll, 1866), Stephane Mallarmé's "Un Coup de Dés" (Mallarmé, 1897), and Guillaume Apollinaire's "Calligrammes" (Apollinaire, 1991), illustrate that British and French poets had been experimenting with shape poems long before the modern era (Draper, 1999).

Most scholars of concrete poetry have characterized it as an international movement. One of the most well-known scholarly texts about concrete poetry, written by US poet Mary Ellen Solt in 1968, organized the extant concrete poetry literature by geographical region, noting particularly active communities in Brazil and Europe. As Draper (1999) observed, an emphasis on shape rather than words enabled concrete poetry "to transcend the regional and national divisions associated with the use of a spoken language" (p. 222). When Swiss poet Eugen Gomringer (as cited in Solt, 1968) wrote his concrete poetry manifesto in 1956, he described the movement as

> International-supranational. It is a significant characteristic of the existential necessity of concrete poetry that creations such as those brought together in this volume began to appear almost simultaneously in Europe and South America . . . I am therefore convinced that concrete poetry is in the process of realizing the idea of a universal poetry. (p. 68)

Indeed, this phenomenon of simultaneous innovations occurring across the globe may be what differentiated the modern concrete poetry movement from the lone poets who created shape poems in the past. By playing with language, manipulating graphic space, and interacting with each other's work, concrete poets from around the globe addressed themes of globalization, transnationalism, and the universality of language in innovative ways (Graber & Rivière, 2017).

In the 1960s, the concrete poetry movement spread to the USA, where poets such as Emmett Williams, Mary Ellen Solt, and Richard Kostelanetz developed their own concrete poetry and wrote anthologies (e.g., Kostelanetz, 1970; Solt, 1968; Williams, 1967) that showcased the existing body of concrete poetry and provided biographical information and commentary about the poets. Williams's 1967 anthology presented a compilation of the work of 70 concrete poets, accompanied by biographical information about the authors, as well as his commentary about the poems.

Solt (1968) extended Williams's work by providing a detailed historical overview of the concrete poetry movement, English translations of manifestos written by leading concrete poets, stunning reproductions of more than 150 concrete poems, informed interpretations of the poems, and a multilingual glossary to help readers understand poems that were written in poets' native languages. Solt's work exemplifies the innovative, international, and visual aspects of concrete poetry.

As previously mentioned, May Swenson's iconographic poetry shares certain characteristics with Solt's concrete poetry. Although she did not identify as a concrete poet, Swenson also theorized about the relationship between word and image. Commenting on her book *Iconographs* (1970), Swenson wrote

> To have material and mold evolve together and become a symbiotic whole. To cause an instant object-to-eye encounter with each poem even before it is read word-after-word. To have simultaneity as well as sequence. To make an existence in space, as well as in time, for the poem. These have been, I suppose, the impulses behind the typed shapes and frames invented for this collection. (p. 86)

One of Swenson's iconographic poems, "How Everything Happens (Based on a Study of the Wave)," ebbs and flows across the page, constrained only by the margins of the page and the limitations of the 1960s typewriter (Spooner, 2006). As Spooner observed, this poem serves as a visual and prosodic representation of a wave, as well as a metaphor for creative writing.

Kostelanetz (1970) added to the extant literature by showcasing roughly 100 poems, most of which had not been published in previous anthologies. As previously noted, Kostelanetz made the distinction between imaged words and worded images when describing the existing body of concrete poetry: "In imaged words, a significant word or phrase is endowed with a visual form, so that language is enhanced through *pictorial* means. In worded images, in contrast, language fills an image, embellishing the shape through linguistic means..." (para. 1). This distinction is important because it demarcates two subgenres of concrete poetry: Imaged words usually consist of a word or a few words (e.g., Robert Indiana's iconic "LOVE" sculpture), whereas worded images are rooted in an image (e.g., Mary Ellen Solt's "Forsythia"). In imaged words, words are often whittled down to their essential letters or syllables; in worded images, the poems are drawn out, like sketches that spill across the page (or multiple pages, as is the case with Mallarmé's "One Toss of the Dice," which spans 21 pages; Poetry Foundation, n.d.).

In the late 1970s, concrete poetry became passé (Bean & McCabe, 2015). According to Perloff (2008), literary critics such as Bayard (1989) pointed out the shortcomings of concrete poetry as seen through the lens of Umberto Eco's 1976 iconic fallacy theory. Essentially, critics questioned the assumption that poems should attempt to fuse form and content. "The 1950s experiment in material poetics was ideologically suspect—too 'pretty,' too empty of 'meaningful' content, too much like advertising copy" (Perloff, 2008, p. 66). As Kostelanetz (2011) reflected in his self-deprecating autobiographical poem, "No one ever thought me in fashion. I failed to win acceptance from powerful literary mobs..." (p. 21). Although Kostelanetz continued to publish his work into the twenty-first century, the movement lost momentum.

In 1996, Kenneth Goldsmith launched UbuWeb, n.d. an online repository of concrete poetry. As Goldsmith (2009) reflected, "There was something formally astonishing about the way that the computer screen and concrete poetry seemed to work naturally together. It seemed a fulfillment of concrete poetry's original premise" (p. 50). Similarly, Bean and McCabe (2015) observed, "The great dreams of the democratization of concrete poetry by poets such as Henri Chopin have become embedded into our everyday activities" (p. 14). With the advent of the personal computer and the Internet, poets and readers were able to create and consume new forms of *digital poetry*, "a genre that fuses crafted language with new media technology and techniques enabled by such equipment" whereby "words are arranged into literal shapes; words show patterns that represent dispersal or displacement of language; or words are combined with images" (Funkhouser, 2007, pp. 318–322). Digital poetry has diverse, constantly evolving forms that range from simple computer-generated texts (e.g., Poem Generator, n.d.); to complex programmable poems and codework (e.g., Cayley, n.d.); to kinetic, multimedia video poems (e.g., Caselli, 2009). Concrete video poems such as Caselli's blur the boundaries between poetry and film, juxtaposing text, images and sound in startlingly original ways.

Perloff (2008) referred to the rebirth of concrete poetry in new media as "arrière-garde" (p. 66): When an avant-garde movement (such as the concrete poetry movement) is no longer a novelty, it is the role of the arrière-garde (in this case, digital poetry repositories such as Moving Poems (n.d.), TED-Ed (n.d.), UbuWeb (n.d.), and Vispo n.d.) to insure its success. Paralleling their predecessors in the 60s and 70s, contemporary arrière-garde scholars Bean and McCabe (2015), Bohn (2011), and Hill and Vassilakis (2012) have published anthologies of concrete and visual poetry in the twenty-first century. Note that Bohn's (2011) definition of visual poetry as "poetry that is meant to be seen" (p. 13) doesn't differentiate visual poetry from concrete poetry in a meaningful way. Perhaps this is because concrete and visual poetry are so closely related: Both practices integrate literature and art. In contrast, Swenson's (1970) statement that iconographic poems "are to be seen, as well as read and heard" (p. 87) suggests that iconographic poets are located closer to the literary end of the continuum (poet-artists), whereas concrete and visual poets are situated closer to the artistic end of the spectrum (artist-poets).

Research poetry and poetic inquiry. Only within the past 25 years has poetry been recognized as an alternative form of representation in social science research. Unlike concrete and iconographic poetry, which have traditionally been male-dominated disciplines—with the notable exceptions of Mary Ellen Solt and May Swenson—research poetry has feminine roots. One of the first scholars to passionately embrace the creative analytic practice of poetic representation was US sociologist Laurel Richardson (1992), who confessed,

> I have breached sociological writing expectations by writing sociology as poetry…By violating the norms of sociological production and dissemination, I have felt the power of those norms, their role in suppressing lived experience, and the exhilaration of writing nonalienating sociology. (p. 126)

Richardson referred to her poem "Louisa May's Story of Her Life" as a "transcript masquerading as a poem/a poem masquerading as a transcript" (p. 127). She described the difficult literary challenge inherent in constructing a poem from a transcript comprised of speech that was bland, unconcretized, and devoid of images, metaphors, and poetic language. Nevertheless, by using spaces and line breaks to capture the rhythm in her informant's voice, Richardson successfully distilled her participant's experience in a poem.

Corinne Glesne (1997) extended Richardson's (1992) work by explicating a method for generating research poems. Glesne, a qualitative methodologist from the US, is perhaps best known for her work on poetic transcription, in which she represented her participant's words from an interview transcript in the form of a poem. Glesne created six poetic transcriptions derived from an interview that she conducted with Dona Juana, an elderly Puerto Rican researcher and educator. She began by conducting a traditional qualitative thematic analysis of the data. Next, she created "poemlike compositions" from the transcribed interview. Her process involved using her interviewee's words (as opposed to the researcher's words) and keeping enough words together to re-present the interviewee's speaking rhythm and speech patterns. In describing poetic transcription as "an amalgamation of science and the literary" (p. 216), Glesne asserted:

> I believe that this amalgamation is useful, not because it produces good art or rigorous science (although it could possibly do both), but because it opens up a spirit of discovery and creation in the researcher, and in the reader, who may begin to think about the process and product of research in very different ways. (p. 216)

Here, Glesne is alluding to two very different, but equally valid, motivations for writing research poems: The heuristic value of generating alternative representations of research findings via research poetry; and the epistemological standpoint of poetic inquiry as a valid way of knowing. Similar to Richardson's (2000) perspective on writing as a method of inquiry, the practice of writing research poetry is not only a way to give voice to one's participants via found poems; it is also a way of finding out about oneself. As Leggo (2005) offered, "Poetry is a way of knowing and being and becoming" (p. 442). In other words, *poetic inquiry* is "a phenomenological and existential choice that extends beyond the use of poetic methods to a way of being in the world" (Prendergast, 2009, para. 18).

In 2002, Canadian education professor Lynn Butler-Kisber built on the work of Richardson and Glesne by employing found poetry to portray the voice of a graduate student named Ann. Butler-Kisber described the process that she used to create found poetry as nonlinear: After viewing videotapes several times to create a "mental kaleidoscope" (p. 233) of the sight and sound of her participant, she "nuggeted" words and phrases from the chained prose. She experimented with words to create rhythms, pauses, emphasis, breath-points, syntax and diction; then played with order and line

1.2 History

breaks to portray the essence of her story. She read her work aloud many times as she refined her initial draft to produce a final version.

In 2006, Canadian theatre professor Monica Prendergast added to the conversation about poetic inquiry by creating found poetry from a review of the literature. She borrowed words from primary source texts and used line breaks, patterns on the page, parentheses, and repetition to reconfigure them as poems. This project emerged from Prendergast's dissertation, which was the first systematic review of the literature related to poetry in research. One visionary characteristic of Prendergast's work is that she later reached out to the authors of the sources that she reviewed and invited them to collaborate with her in what became the International Symposium on Poetic Inquiry.

From 2007 to 2022, an invisible college of research poets from around the world gathered biennially at the International Symposium on Poetic Inquiry (ISPI). First organized at the University of British Columbia, Canada, by Monica Prendergast and Carl Leggo, the symposium became a place where scholars could share their poetic inquiry. Subsequently, six anthologies (Galvin & Prendergast, 2016; Honein & McKeon, 2023; Prendergast et al., 2009a; Sameshima et al., 2018; Thomas et al., 2012; Van Rooyen et al., 2023) and five special issues of scholarly journals (Butler-Kisber, 2010; Faulkner, 2018a; Galvin & Prendergast, 2012; Guiney Yallop et al., 2014; and Prendergast et al., 2009b) have been published to disseminate poetic inquiry from these symposia. As the special issues were published in peer-reviewed, online, open access journals such as *Art/Research International, Creative Approaches to Research, Educational Insights, in education,* and *LEARNING Landscapes,* diverse readers can access the information, regardless of their socioeconomic status, institutional affiliation, or geographic location. At the 2022 symposium in Cape Town, South Africa, nearly 150 scholars, poets, and performance artists from Australia, Canada, New Zealand, South Africa, the UK, and the USA presented a diverse array of poetic inquiry and research poetry. Over the past 15 years, members of the poetic inquiry community have also participated in McGill University's Artful Inquiry Research Group Symposium, as well as the American Educational Research Association Annual Meeting and the International Congress on Qualitative Inquiry, both of which have Arts-Based Research Special Interest Groups. In addition, *The Handbook of Arts-Based Research* (Leavy, 2018) and arts-based research primer *Method Meets Art* (Leavy, 2009, 2015, 2020) have featured chapters about poetic inquiry.

In 2009, US communication professor Sandra Faulkner wrote a book about research poetry entitled *Poetry as Method*, which explored the connection between social science and poetry. Unlike the ISPI anthologies, Faulkner's text was a single-authored methods book about writing research poems. She framed her subject as research poetry, rather than poetic inquiry, the term used by the ISPI anthology editors. In her book, she described the practice of writing poetry as a method for representing research findings, presented examples of various forms of research poetry, and offered suggestions for evaluating the quality of research poems, as well as writing exercises for aspiring research poets. Faulkner's extensive treatment of evaluating research poetry (see also Faulkner, 2007) provided scholars with a helpful set of criteria for discerning what constitutes effective research poetry. In the second edition of her text, Faulkner (2020) changed her focus from research poetry to poetic inquiry, expanding her discussion of poetry as a form of representation to include a broader conceptualization of poetry as/in/for inquiry (Faulkner, 2018b). Faulkner (2018b) defined poetic inquiry as "the use of poetry crafted from research endeavors, either before project analysis, as a project analysis, and/or poetry that is part of or that constitutes an entire research project" (p. 210). From this perspective, research poems can inform a research project, be part of the analytic process, or represent the research findings as a whole or in part. As Vincent (2018) observed, there is no one exclusive way to conduct poetic inquiry.

Faulkner (2009) acknowledged that "the label 'poet' is problematic, as one can self-publish a book, teach poetry, and that still doesn't make one a poet" (p. 66). Inherent in this distinction is the idea that not all research poetry adheres to aesthetic criteria that inform the art and craft of writing poetry. As Richardson (2000), Percer (2002), and Faulkner (2007) have asserted, we need to establish (and periodically revisit) criteria to evaluate the quality of research poetry. Richardson identified substantive contribution, aesthetic merit, reflexivity, impact, and expression of a reality as characteristics that can be used to evaluate social science art forms. Faulkner highlighted artistic concentration, embodied experience, discovery and/or surprise, conditionality, narrative truth, and transformation as criteria for judging the success of research poetry. Percer advocated for a critical adoption of poetry in research, whereby scholars are asked to state a precise rationale for using poetic representations and to question whether poetry is appropriate for meeting the goals of their research.

Faulkner (2020) recognized the difficulty inherent in attempting to achieve credibility and rigor in both poetry and research at the same time. She also acknowledged the "caveat of constraint," namely that "criteria limit alternative forms of research writing by constraining freedom and possibility" (p. 150). It is perhaps because of these challenges that Lahman and Richard (2014) advocated for "good enough" research poetry:

> With the understanding that learning to write well, both in prose and verse, takes time, training, and practice; we advocate for the space to engage in writing good enough research poetry while the research poet hones her craft. (p. 352)

Lahman et al.'s (2011) position that researchers should be encouraged to experiment with words reflects a process-oriented philosophy that encourages arts-based researchers to create new forms of representation. Lahman's commitment to this philosophy is evidenced by the abundant and creative nature of her scholarship: In a recent chapter about "poemish research representations," Lahman (2022) provided exemplars of over a dozen different forms of research poetry that she has published over time. As Lahman demonstrates, when we allow ourselves to focus on the artistic process, rather than feeling pressured to produce a professional product, we develop curiosity and creativity as habits of mind (Lapum & Hume, 2015).

One emerging area of poetic inquiry that reflects curiosity and creativity is digital poetic inquiry. In the same way that technological advances have transformed the

1.2 History

landscape of concrete poetry, digital poetry has made inroads in the field of poetic inquiry. Kedrick James (2009a) is perhaps the first scholar who employed digital poetry as a method of poetic inquiry. For his dissertation, James created cut-up poems that he generated from spam email using a process similar to erasure or black-out poetry, in which "the cut-up becomes poetically resonant by procedurally eliminating information in the text from which it is culled" (James, 2009a, p. 181). He employed both chance-generated procedures and selective editing to reduce and repurpose electronic junk mail into an artful installation of research poems.

In 2015, Adrian Schoone conducted dissertation research about the lived experiences of alternative education tutors in New Zealand. Schoone employed James's (2009a, 2009b) cut-up method, kinetic sculpture, and digital photography to create 2- and 3-dimensional concrete poems that represented his participants' voices. Because Schoone photographed the poems, then edited the photographs on his computer, I characterize his work as digital research poetry here; in Chap. 3, I will treat his work in greater depth as an exemplar of concrete research poetry.

The most recent example of digital poetic inquiry is Susan Cannon's (2018) article about the transcription process. In her paper, she applied Goldsmith's (2011) uncreative writing exercises to convert qualitative interview data from her original transcription to various media, including collage, a musical translation of the audio, screenshots of the image produced by the recording software, a .txt file, a word count, her participant's unrecorded words hand-stitched on cloth, a .txt file of a photograph of her participant, an open iteration, and a rev.com transcription. She created a series of self-portraits and research poems that reflected on processes of "re/search and re/presentation" (p. 1) related to the transcription process.

Another emerging area of poetic inquiry is installation art (Lapum, 2018). Because installation art typically involves the display of multiple forms of media in a physical space, it offers a unique opportunity to engage audience members. As Lapum observed, installation art has traditionally been seen as a method of disseminating research findings. Lapum et al. (2014) created an art installation entitled, "The 7024th Patient," which employed poetry and photographs to chronicle patients' experiences with open-heart surgery and recovery. The authors employed narrative methodology to analyze attendees' open-ended comments and focus group data. Attendees reported that the exhibit immersed them in patients' experiences, which prompted self-reflection. Lapum (2018) concluded that installation art is a high-impact method of disseminating research findings to the public because it creates experiential encounters that evoke emotions, challenge taken-for-granted assumptions, prompt critical reflection, and invite dialogue between researchers and audience members.

1.3 Summary

As I have described in this chapter, concrete poetry, iconographic poetry, poetic inquiry, and research poetry have strong intellectual traditions. Concrete and iconographic poetry fuse literature and art, whereas research poetry fuses literature and the social sciences. Each genre has multiple forms that exist on a continuum: Iconographic poetry is closer to literature than art, whereas visual poetry and concrete poetry are closer to art than literature; poetic inquiry is closer to literature than social science, while research poetry is closer to social science than literature. (See Fig. 1.5 for a visual representation of iconographic research poetry as it relates to art, science, and literature.) Each genre originated as an avant-garde movement, resuscitated by contemporary arrière-garde movements. Across genres, contemporary movements have democratized access to their material via websites and online open access journals. Each genre is international, with active communities around the globe. Historically, concrete poetry and shaped poetry have been male-dominated forms of writing, whereas research poetry and poetic inquiry are typically pink-collared methodologies. Although the intellectual camps share many characteristics, they have traditionally been separated by disciplinary boundaries. In fusing concrete poetry, iconographic poetry, research poetry, and poetic inquiry to propose iconographic research poetry, a new form of inquiry that spans literature, art, and the social sciences, I aspire to spark a conversation among scholars housed within these previously siloed disciplines.

1.4 Why Iconographic Research Poetry?

As I have argued elsewhere (i.e., Meyer, 2017), there are a number of benefits to using iconographic poetic structures in research poetry. (See Table 1.1.) First, iconographic research poetry reflects the principle of crystallization (Ellingson, 2009; Richardson, 2000) in which the act of representation is accomplished via multiple genres. Whether employed as an alternative to a traditional literature review or a results section, iconographic research poems have the potential to transform data into art, providing greater insight than traditional qualitative analysis alone. Second, because word-images convey metaphoric structure through visual cues, iconographic poetry is a powerful device for representing metaphors. Third, because iconographic poetry enlists visual images to help shape the reader's interpretation, it may be more easily digested than traditional research findings and conventional forms of poetry. Therefore, it offers a vehicle for translating scholarly research into a more accessible format that can be appreciated by both scholars and community members. Finally, as a form of poetic inquiry, iconographic research poetry can enhance teacher-scholar-students' creativity. For these reasons, iconographic research poetry is a promising methodological innovation for arts-based researchers who are interested in issues such as crystallization, metaphor, representation, and public research.

1.5 Preview of the Book

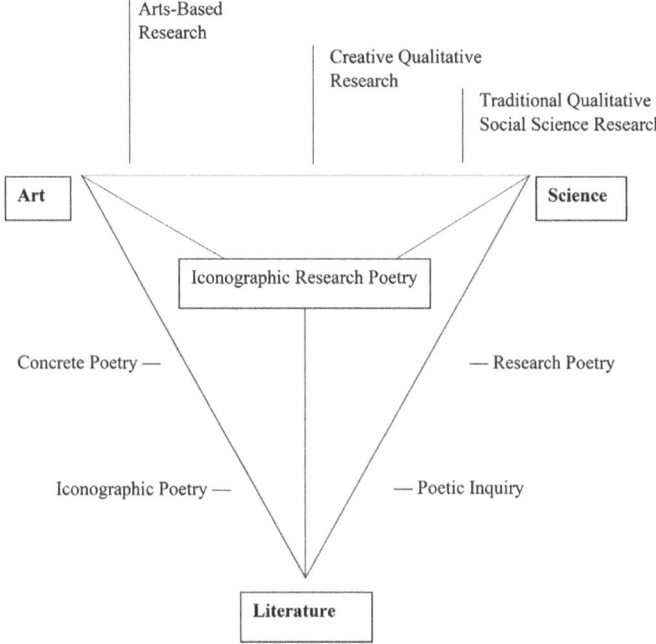

Fig. 1.5 Triangular prism: art, science, literature, and iconographic research poetry

Table 1.1 Advantages of concrete research poetry

Concrete research poems can
1. Transform data into art
2. Provide greater insight than traditional qualitative analysis alone
3. Offer a powerful device for representing metaphors
4. Translate scholarly research into an accessible format that can be appreciated by both scholars and community members
5. Invite creativity into teacher-scholar-students' lives

1.5 Preview of the Book

Chapter 2 offers a detailed description of the methods that can be used to create and design iconographic research poetry. I begin by locating iconographic research poetry on the qualitative continuum (Ellingson, 2009). Next, I present an overview of iterative thematic analysis (Tracy, 2013, 2020) and metaphor analysis (Tracy et al., 2006), two qualitative analytic methods. Drawing from the extant literature in research poetry and poetic inquiry (e.g., Ellingson, 2011; Faulkner, 2009, 2020; Glesne, 1997; Prendergast, 2012), concrete, iconographic, and visual poetry (e.g., Bohn, 2011; Kostelanetz, 1970; Solt, 1968; Swenson, 1970), as well as germinal work in iconographic research poetry (previously referred to as concrete research poetry by

Meyer, 2017; Miller, 2019; Schoone, 2020, 2021), I explicate the processes by which data can be represented in the form of iconographic research poetry. Next, I provide a step-by-step description of strategies that researchers can use to create iconographic research poetry from qualitative data. Specifically, I describe my methods of creating iconographic research poems with word processing software and graphic design programs using typed text, clip art or icons, and layered text and images. I discuss the importance of soliciting member reflections from participants and artist-poets. At the end of the chapter, I offer writing exercises designed to help aspiring iconographic research poets exercise their poetic imagination. For example, I ask readers to re-analyze an existing qualitative data set with the methods I have previously described. I invite qualitative researchers to make their first foray into iconographic research poetry by conducting a metaphor analysis, selecting a visual image to represent the metaphor, and creating an iconographic research poem with word processing software.

Chapter 3 provides a review of extant exemplars of concrete and iconographic research poetry. I trace the development of concrete and iconographic research poetry in recent journal articles, book chapters, and books (e.g., Lahman & DeOliveira, 2021; Lahman et al., 2019; Meyer, 2017; Miller, 2019; Penwarden & Schoone, 2021; Schoone, 2018, 2019, 2020). In addition to describing and interpreting recently published exemplars, I share some previously unpublished iconographic ekphrastic research poetry (e.g., "Grounds for a Miracle Backstory") that has promising implications for collaborative arts-based inquiry. Following my review, I engage in a reflexive examination of ethical tensions that I experienced as a non-Native scholar writing about Native artists and their works of art. At the end of the chapter, I offer exercises designed to help writers develop their poetic inquiry practice. Specifically, I elaborate on techniques suggested by creative writing coaches (e.g., Cameron, 1992; Davis, 2008) and meditation teachers (e.g., Smith, n.d.), who instruct writers to enhance their creativity by writing morning pages, going on artist dates, practicing yoga poetry, and engaging in walking meditation.

Chapter 4 explores techniques for integrating iconographic research poetry in the classroom. I begin by providing an overview of arts-based research pedagogy (Barone & Eisner, 2006; Bresler, 2018; Dixon & Senior, 2009). Next, I describe pedagogical innovations that embrace research poetry (e.g., Benton & Russell, 2016; Guyas & Keys, 2009; Jacob & Kincaid, 2018; Lahman & DeOliveira, 2021; Lapum & Hume, 2015; Meyer & Helmer, in press). Finally, I offer readers a toolkit that they can use to incorporate iconographic research poetry into their qualitative research courses. In the toolkit, I adapt techniques developed by writers who teach (e.g., Addonizio, 2009; Cohen, 2009; Padgett, 2000) in an effort to generate poetry-centered exercises for the classroom. By prompting students to create a broadside (a poem incorporating an image), a shape poem with line breaks, or a found poem shaped like a calligram, qualitative research instructors can cultivate creativity in the research methods classroom and encourage students to begin thinking about concepts like crystallization and alternative representation of findings (Ellingson, 2009; Richardson, 2000).

Chapter 5 offers a summary of the book, as well as a critical discussion about the limitations of iconographic research poetry and the implications of employing various media to represent one's research findings. I generate directions for future research, citing digital concrete poetry (e.g., Caselli, 2009) and installation art and poetry (e.g., Lapum et al., 2014) as inspiration for future experiments in iconographic research poetry. In addition, I initiate a self-reflexive discussion about how this exercise in poetic inquiry—the process of writing a book about iconographic research poetry—has changed me. This reflection, continued in the postscript, explores what living poetically in community means to me. By reviewing literature about poetic inquiry (Leggo, 2008; Prendergast, 2009; Sameshima et al., 2018) and identity (Clarke, 2014; Sjollema & Yuen, 2018), I explore how the practice of poetic inquiry can be a constant source of discovery and renewal for teacher-scholars. Toward this end, I encourage readers to nurture the spirit of curiosity and playfulness that is inherent in us all by developing a regular writing practice, engaging in creative writing exercises, experimenting with poetic inquiry and iconographic research poetry in their scholarship, and integrating poetry-centered exercises in their teaching. This chapter ends with a list of additional resources, including scholarly books, journal articles, videos, digital archives, museum websites, and children's books that readers can consult to learn more about concrete and digital poetry, as well as poetic inquiry.

References

Addonizio, K. (2009). *Ordinary genius*. W. W. Norton & Company.
Apollinaire, G. (1991). *Calligrammes*. University of California Press.
Barone, T., & Eisner, E. (2006). Arts-based educational research. In J. Green, G. Camilli, P. Elmore, A. Skukauskaite, & E. Grace (Eds.), *Handbook of complementary methods in education research* (pp. 95–110). Lawrence Erlbaum Associates.
Bayard, C. (1989). *The new poetics in Canada and Quebec*. University of Toronto Press.
Bean, V., & McCabe, B. (2015). *The new concrete: Visual poetry in the 21st century*. Hayward Publishing.
Benton, A., & Russell, A. (2016). "Using the other side of my brain": Creativity in the research classroom. *Journal of Poetry Therapy, 29*(3), 147–159. https://doi.org/10.1080/08893675.2016.1200257
Bertram. (2021). LOVE sculpture in arts park, New Castle, Indiana [Photograph]
Bohn, W. (2011). *Reading visual poetry*. Fairleigh Dickinson University Press.
Bresler, L. (2018). Aesthetic-based research as pedagogy: The interplay of knowing and unknowing toward expanded seeing. In P. Leavy (Ed.), *Handbook of arts-based research* (pp. 649–672). Guilford Press.
Butler-Kisber, L. (2002). Artful portrayals in qualitative inquiry: The road to found poetry and beyond. *The Alberta Journal of Educational Research, 48*(3), 229–239. http://www.ajer.ca/
Butler-Kisber, L. (Ed.). (2010). Poetry and education: Possibilities and practices [Special issue]. *LEARNING Landscapes, 4*(1). https://www.learninglandscapes.ca/
Cameron, J. (1992). *The artist's way: A spiritual path to higher creativity*. G P. Putnam's Sons.
Cannon, S. O. (2018). Teasing transcription: Iterations in the liminal space between voice and text. *Qualitative Inquiry, 24*(8), 571–582. https://doi.org/10.1177/1077800417742412
Carr, J. (2003). Poetic expressions of vigilance. *Qualitative Health Research, 13*(9), 1324–1331. https://doi.org/10.1177/1049732303254018

Carroll, L. (1866). The mouse's tail/tale. *The University of Michigan Library Online Exhibits.* https://www.lib.umich.edu/online-exhibits/exhibits/show/-curiouser-and-curiouser----ex/the-mouse-s-tail-tale

Caselli, C. (2009, 23 June). *Cinco poemas concretos.* [Video poem]. Moving Poems. https://movingpoems.com/2009/06/cinco-poemas-concretos-five-concrete-poems/

Cayley, J. (n.d.). John Cayley's personal website. http://shadoof.net

Clarke, C. (2014). Liminal lives: Navigating the spaces between (poet and scholar). *In Education, 20*(2), 103–120.

Cohen, S. (2009). *Writing the life poetic: An invitation to read & write poetry.* Writer's Digest Books.

Davis, J. (2008). *The journey from the center to the page: Yoga philosophies and practices as muse for authentic writing.* Monkfish Book Publishing Co.

Dixon, M., & Senior, K. (2009). Traversing theory and transgressing academic discourses: Arts-based research in teacher education. *International Journal of Education & the Arts, 10*(24), 1–21. http://www.ijea.org/v10n24

Draper, R. (1999). *An introduction to twentieth-century poetry in English.* St Martin's Press.

Drury, J. (1995). *The poetry dictionary.* Story Press.

Ellingson, L. (2009). *Engaging crystallization in qualitative research: An introduction.* Sage.

Ellingson, L. (2011). The poetics of professionalism among dialysis technicians. *Health Communication, 26*(1), 1–12. https://doi.org/10.1080/10410236.2011.527617

Faulkner, S. (2005). Method: Six poems. *Qualitative Inquiry, 11*(6), 941–949. https://doi.org/10.1177/1077800405276813

Faulkner, S. (2007). Concern with craft: Using *Ars Poetica* as criteria for reading research poetry. *Qualitative Inquiry, 13*(2), 218–234. https://doi.org/10.1177/1077800406295636

Faulkner, S. (2009). *Poetry as method: Reporting research through verse.* Left Coast Press.

Faulkner, S. (Ed.). (2018a). Poetry and social justice [Special issue]. *Art/Research International, 3*(1). https://journals.library.ualberta.ca/ari/index.php/ari/index

Faulkner, S. (2018b). Poetic inquiry: Poetry as/in/for social research. In P. Leavy (Ed.), *Handbook of arts-based research* (pp. 208–230). Guilford Press.

Faulkner, S. (2020). *Poetic inquiry: Craft, method, and practice* (2nd ed.). Routledge.

Funkhouser, C. (2007). Digital poetry: A look at generative, visual, and interconnected possibilities in its first four decades. In R. Siemens, S. Schreibman, & A. Liu (Eds.), *A companion to digital literary studies* (pp. 318–335). Wiley-Blackwell.

Furman, R. (2006). Poetic forms and structures in qualitative health research. *Qualitative Health Research, 16*(4), 560–566. https://doi.org/10.1177/1049732306286819

Galvin, K. & Prendergast, M. (Eds.). (2012). Poetic inquiry [Special issue]. *Creative Approaches to Research, 5*(2). http://creativeapproachestoresearch.net/publications/creative-approaches-to-research/

Galvin, K., & Prendergast, M. (2016). *Poetic inquiry II—Seeing, caring, understanding: Using poetry as and for inquiry.* Sense Publishers.

Glesne, C. (1997). That rare feeling: Re-presenting research through poetic transcription. *Qualitative Inquiry, 3*(2), 202–221. https://doi.org/10.1177/107780049700300204

Goldsmith, K. (2009). The bride stripped bare: Nude media and the dematerialization of Tony Curtis. In A. Morris & T. Swiss (Eds.), *New media poetics: Contexts, technotexts, and theories* (pp. 49–64). The MIT Press.

Goldsmith, K. (2011). *Uncreative writing: Managing language in the digital age.* Columbia University Press.

Gomringer, E. (1968). *The book of hours and constellations.* Something Else Press, Inc.

Graber, L., & Rivière, H. (2017, April 5). Concrete poets played with language to dissolve boundaries on an international scale. *The Iris.* http://blogs.getty.edu/iris/the-borderless-wordplay-of-concrete-poetry/

Guiney Yallop, J., Wiebe, S., & Faulkner, S. (Eds.). (2014). The practices of poetic inquiry [Special issue]. *In education, 20*(2). https://ineducation.ca/ineducation/issue/view/2

References

Guyas, A. S., & Keys, K. (2009). Arts-based educational research as a site for emerging pedagogy and developing mentorship. *Visual Arts Research, 35*(2), 24–39. https://www.jstor.org/stable/20715500

Herbert, G. (1633). *Easter wings*. [Poem]. Poetry Foundation. https://www.poetryfoundation.org/poems/44361/easter-wings

Hill, C., & Vassilakis, N. (2012). *The last vispo anthology: Visual poetry 1998–2008*. Fantagraphics Books.

Hollander, J. (1967). *Types of shape*. McClelland and Stewart Ltd.

Hollander, J. (1975). *Vision and resonance: Two senses of poetic form*. Oxford University Press.

Holman Jones, S. (2011). Lost and found. *Text and Performance Quarterly, 31*(4), 322–341. https://doi.org/10.1080/10462937.2011.602709

Honein, N., & McKeon, M. (2023). *Reclaiming lands, languages, and belongings: A poetic celebration*. Vernon Press.

International Symposium on Poetic Inquiry (n.d.). https://www.poeticinquiry.ca/

Jacob, F., & Kincaid, S. (2018). *Poetry across the curriculum: New methods of writing intensive pedagogy for US community college and undergraduate education*. Brill | Sense.

James, K. (2009a). *Writing post-person: Literacy, poetics, and sustainability in the age of disposable information* (Doctoral dissertation, University of British Columbia).

James, K. (2009b). Cut-up consciousness and talking trash: Poetic inquiry and the spambot's text. In M. Prendergast, C. Leggo, & P. Sameshima (Eds.), *Poetic inquiry: Vibrant voices in the social sciences* (pp. 59–74). Sense Publishers.

Kostelanetz, R. (1970). *Imaged words & worded images*. Outerbridge & Dienstfrey.

Kostelanetz, R. (2011). Memoir of my failures. *Review of Contemporary Fiction, 31*(1), 20–23.

Lahman, M. (2022). Poemish research representations. In M. Lahman (Ed.), *Writing and representing qualitative research* (pp. 207–264). Sage.

Lahman, M., & DeOliveira, B. (2021). Poetry spheres, flower poems: A dimensional poetry experience. *Qualitative Inquiry, 27*(5), 622–625. https://doi.org/10.1177/1077800420941050

Lahman, M., & Richard, V. M. (2014). Appropriated poetry: Archival poetry in research. *Qualitative Inquiry, 20*(3), 344–355. https://doi.org/10.1177/1077800413489272

Lahman, M., Rodriguez, K., Richard, V., Geist, M., Schende, R., & Graglia, P. (2011). (Re)forming research poetry. *Qualitative Inquiry, 17*(9), 887–896. https://doi.org/10.1177/1077800411423219

Lahman, M., Teman, E., & Richard, V. (2019). IRB as poetry. *Qualitative Inquiry, 25*(2), 200–214. https://doi.org/10.1177/10778004177445

Lapum, J. (2018). Installation art: The voyage never ends. In P. Leavy (Ed.), *Handbook of arts-based research* (pp. 377–395). Guilford Press.

Lapum, J., & Hume, S. (2015). Teaching qualitative research: Fostering student curiosity through an arts-informed pedagogy. *The Qualitative Report, 20*(8), 1221–1233. http://www.nova.edu/ssss/QR/QR20/8/lapum2.pdf

Lapum, J. L., Liu, L., Church, K., Yau, T. M., Ruttonsha, P., Matthews David, A., & Retta, B. (2014). Arts-informed research dissemination in the health sciences: An evaluation of peoples' responses to "The 7,024th Patient" art installation. *SAGE Open, 4*(1), 2158244014524211.

Leavy, P. (2009). *Method meets art: Arts-based research practice*. Guilford Press.

Leavy, P. (2015). *Method meets art: Arts-based research practice*. (2nd ed.). Guilford Press.

Leavy, P. (2018). Introduction to arts-based research. In P. Leavy (Ed.), *Handbook of arts-based research* (pp. 3–21). Guilford Press.

Leavy, P. (2020). *Method meets art: Arts-based research practice*. (3rd ed.). Guilford Press.

Leggo, C. (2005). The heart of pedagogy: On poetic knowing and living. *Teachers and Teaching: Theory and Practice, 11*(5), 439–455. https://doi.org/10.1080/13450600500238436

Leggo, C. (2008). Astonishing silence: Knowing in poetry. In J.G. Knowles, & A. L. Cole, A. L. (Eds.), *Handbook of the arts in qualitative research* (pp. 165-174). Sage.

Mallarmé, S. (1897). *One toss of the dice*. [Poem]. UbuWeb. https://www.ubu.com/historical/mallarme/dice.html

Meyer, M. (2017). Concrete research poetry: A visual representation of metaphor. *Art/Research International: A Transdisciplinary Journal, 2*(1), 32–57. https://doi.org/10.18432/R2KS6F

Meyer, M., & Helmer, K. (in press). From "I am not a creative person" to "maybe I am a little artistic": Arts-informed pedagogy, experiential learning, and collaborative research in the creative organizational culture classroom. In F. Fovet (Ed.) *Implementing transformative student-centered pedagogies in the neoliberal academy: Constraints and opportunities*. CSMFL Publications.

Miller, E. (2019). Creating research poetry: A nursing home example. In A. Humble & M. Radina (Eds.), *How qualitative data analysis happens: Moving beyond 'themes emerged'* (pp. 18–33). Routledge.

Moving Poems (n.d.) *The best poetry videos on the web.* https://movingpoems.com/

Padgett, R. (2000). *The straight line: Writings on poetry and poets.* The University of Michigan Press.

Pappne Demecs, I., & Miller, E. (2019). Woven narratives: A craft encounter with tapestry weaving in a residential aged care facility. *Art/Research International: A Transdisciplinary Journal, 4*(9), 256–286. https://doi.org/10.18432/ari29399

Penwarden, S., & Schoone, A. (2021). The pull of words: Reliving a poetry symposium through found poetry. *Art/Research International: A Transdisciplinary Journal, 6*(2), 347–368. https://doi.org/10.18432/ari29572

Percer, L. H. (2002). Going beyond the demonstrable range in educational scholarship: Exploring the intersections of poetry and research. *The Qualitative Report, 7*(2). http://www.nova.edu/ssss/QR/QR7-2/hayespercer.html

Perloff, M. (2008). Writing as re-writing: Concrete poetry as arrière garde. *Interdisciplinary Humanities, 25*(1), 66–89.

Poetry Foundation. (n.d.). *Stéphane Mallarmé.* https://www.poetryfoundation.org/poets/stephane-mallarme

Poem Generator. (n.d.). https://www.poem-generator.org.uk/

Prendergast, M. (2004). Inquiry and poetry: Haiku on audience and performance in education. *Language and Literacy, 6*(1). https://doi.org/10.20360/G2RK52

Prendergast, M. (2006) Found poetry as literature review. *Qualitative Inquiry 12*(2) 369-388 https://doi.org/10.1177/1077800405284601.

Prendergast, M. (2009). Poetic inquiry is … 29 ways of looking at poetry as qualitative research. *Educational Insights, 13*(3). http://einsights.ogpr.educ.ubc.ca/v13n03/intro/prendergast.html

Prendergast, M. (2012). Education and/as art: A found poetry suite. *International Journal of Education & the Arts, 13*(2), 1–18.

Prendergast, M., Leggo, C., & Sameshima, P. (2009a). *Poetic inquiry: Vibrant voices in the social sciences.* Sense Publishers.

Prendergast, M., Leggo, C., & Sameshima, P. (Eds.). (2009b). Poetic inquiry [Special issue]. *Educational Insights, 13*(3). http://einsights.ogpr.educ.ubc.ca/v13n03/toc.html

Richardson, L. (1992). The consequences of poetic representation: Writing the other, rewriting the self. In C. Ellis & M. Flaherty (Eds.), *Investigating subjectivity: Research on lived experience* (pp. 125–140). Sage.

Richardson, L. (2000). Writing: A method of inquiry. In N. Denzin & Y. Lincoln (Eds.), *Handbook of qualitative research* (2nd ed., pp. 923–943). Sage.

Sameshima, P., Fidyk, A., James, K., & Leggo, C. (2018). *Poetic inquiry: Enchantment of place.* Vernon Press.

Schoone, A. (2015). *Constellations of alternative education tutor essences* [Doctoral thesis, University of Auckland, Auckland, New Zealand]. Library and Learning Services. https://researchspace.auckland.ac.nz/handle/2292/27374

Schoone, A. (2018). The found poem as a constellation. In P. Sameshima, A. Fidyk, K. James, & C. Leggo (Eds.), *Poetic inquiry: Enchantment of place* (pp. 271–280). Vernon Press.

Schoone, A. (2019). An ekphrastic review of Ilona Pappne Demecs and Evonne Miller's "Woven narratives: A craft encounter with tapestry weaving in a residential aged care facility." *Art/*

Research International: A Transdisciplinary Journal, 4(1), 429–432. https://journals.library.ualberta.ca/ari/index.php/ari/issue/view/1943/showToc

Schoone, A. (2020). *Constellations of alternative education tutors: A poetic inquiry*. Springer. https://www.springer.com/gp/book/9783030354947

Schoone, A. (2021). Can concrete poems fly? Setting data free in a performance of visual enactment. *Qualitative Inquiry, 27*(1), 129–135. https://doi.org/10.1177/1077800419884976

Sjollema, S., & Yuen, F. (2017). Evocative words and ethical crafting: Poetic representation in leisure research. *Leisure Sciences, 39*(2), 109–125. https://doi.org/10.1080/01490400.2016.1151845

Sjollema, S., & Yuen, F. (2018). Poetic representation, reflexivity and the recursive turn. In P. Sameshima, A. Fidyk, K. James, & C. Leggo (Eds.), *Poetic inquiry: Enchantment of place* (pp. 59–68). Vernon Press.

Smith, S. (n.d.) *Walking meditation practice*. Contemplative Mind. https://www.contemplativemind.org/practices/tree/walking-meditation

Solt, M. (1968). *Concrete poetry: A world view*. Indiana University Press.

Spooner, M. (2006). How everything happens: Notes on May Swenson's theory of writing. In P. Crumbley & P. M. Gantt (Eds.), *Body my house: May Swenson's work and life* (pp. 157–180). Utah State University Press.

Swenson, M. (1970). *Iconographs*. Charles Scribner's Sons.

TED-Ed. (n.d.) *There's a poem for that*. https://www.youtube.com/playlist?list=PLJicmE8fK0Egxi0hgy5Tw-NFyLcpJ4bzJ

Thomas, S., Cole, A., & Stewart, S. (2012). *The art of poetic inquiry*. Backalong Books.

Tracy, S. (2013). *Qualitative research methods: Collecting evidence, crafting analysis, communicating impact*. Wiley.

Tracy, S. (2020). *Qualitative research methods: Collecting evidence, crafting analysis, communicating impact*. (2nd ed.). Wiley.

Tracy, S., Lutgen-Sandvik, P., & Alberts, J. (2006). Nightmares, demons, and slaves: Exploring the painful metaphors of workplace bullying. *Management Communication Quarterly, 20*(2), 148–185. https://doi.org/10.1177/0893318906291980

Traver, A. (2018). Contextualizing math and poetry in community college courses: Impacts and implications in introduction to sociology. In F. Jacob & S. Kincaid (Eds.), *Poetry across the curriculum* (pp. 161–173). Brill | Sense.

Ubuweb. (n.d.). *UbuWeb: All avant-garde*. http://www.ubu.com/

Van Rooyen, H., D'Abdon, R., Hough, A., Ndlovu, D., Pithouse-Morgan, K., Pete, M., Prince, B., & Sliep, Y. (2023). *Voices unbound: Poems of the Eighth International Symposium on Poetic Inquiry*. African Sun Press.

Vincent, A. (2018). Is there a definition? Ruminating on poetic inquiry, strawberries, and the continued growth of the field. *Art/ Research International: A Transdisciplinary Journal, 3*(2), 48–76. https://doi.org/10.18432/ari29356

Vispo. (n.d.) *Vispo~Langu(im)age: Experimental visual poetry, literary programming, and essays on new media by Jim Andrews*. https://vispo.com/index2.html

Williams, E. (1967). *An anthology of concrete poetry*. Something Else Press.

Open Access This chapter is licensed under the terms of the Creative Commons Attribution 4.0 International License (http://creativecommons.org/licenses/by/4.0/), which permits use, sharing, adaptation, distribution and reproduction in any medium or format, as long as you give appropriate credit to the original author(s) and the source, provide a link to the Creative Commons license and indicate if changes were made.

The images or other third party material in this chapter are included in the chapter's Creative Commons license, unless indicated otherwise in a credit line to the material. If material is not included in the chapter's Creative Commons license and your intended use is not permitted by statutory regulation or exceeds the permitted use, you will need to obtain permission directly from the copyright holder.

Chapter 2
Methods: Designing Iconographic Research Poetry

Abstract In this chapter, the author provides a detailed description of the methods that can be used to create and design iconographic research poetry. After exploring the paradigms that inform iconographic research poetry, she offers a step-by-step description of analytic strategies that researchers can use to generate iconographic research poetry from qualitative data. Drawing from the extant literature in qualitative analysis, research poetry, and concrete and iconographic poetry, the author explicates the processes by which qualitative researchers can represent data in the form of iconographic research poetry. She presents three exemplars to illustrate the techniques that she describes. The author concludes the chapter by offering writing exercises designed to encourage readers to experiment with iconographic research poetry.

Keywords ABR methods · Arts-based educational research (ABER) · Arts-based research (ABR) · Iconographic research poetry · Metaphor analysis · Qualitative analysis · Research poetry

This chapter provides a detailed description of the methods that can be used to create and design iconographic research poetry. As Butler-Kisber (2010) argued, "It is imperative that researchers try to find ways to share our processes with each other" (p. 95). My goal is to provide an explanation that is clear and complete enough that other researchers can use it to replicate my procedures and apply them to create their own iconographic research poems. However, I do not mean to suggest that my method is the only method or the best method for generating iconographic research poems. Indeed, I would be remiss not to invoke Glesne's (1997) caveat: "The process described here is not the way to do poetic transcription; rather, it is one way" (p. 205).

I begin this chapter by locating my methodological approach on the qualitative continuum (Ellingson, 2009). Next, I offer a step-by-step description of analytic strategies that researchers can use to generate iconographic research poetry from qualitative data. I rely on qualitative analysis techniques described by scholars such as Charmaz (2006), Ellingson (2009), Lindlof and Taylor (2011), Malvini Redden et al. (2013), Tracy (2013, 2020), and Tracy et al. (2006). Next, I draw from the extant literature in research poetry and poetic inquiry (e.g., Ellingson, 2011; Faulkner, 2009, 2020; Glesne, 1997; Prendergast, 2012), concrete, iconographic, and visual poetry (e.g., Bohn, 2011; Kostelanetz, 1970; Solt, 1968; Swenson, 1970), and concrete and iconographic research poetry (Meyer, 2017; Miller, 2019; Schoone, 2018), to explicate the processes by which qualitative researchers can represent data in the form of iconographic research poetry. I present three exemplars to illustrate the techniques that I describe. At the end of the chapter, I offer writing exercises designed to encourage readers to experiment with iconographic research poetry.

2.1 The Qualitative Continuum

Before launching into a detailed description of the methods used to create iconographic research poetry, I would like to provide some background about the nature of the *paradigm*, or worldview, that informs my approach. I think of paradigms as meta-theoretical or meta-methodological perspectives shared by a community of scholars. It is important for researchers to contemplate where their research fits within a particular paradigm; in doing so, they may uncover unquestioned assumptions underlying their work.

Over time and across disciplines, methodologists have created different typologies for the paradigms that undergird social science research (e.g., Baxter & Babbie, 2004; Creswell & Poth, 2018; Deetz, 2001; Denzin & Lincoln, 2018; Frey et al., 2000; Smith, 1988; Tracy, 2020). These approaches, which include, but are not limited to positivist, postpositivist, interpretivist, critical, and postmodern/-structural perspectives, are often contrasted in terms of assumptions about ontology (the nature of reality), epistemology (ways of knowing), axiology (the role of values in research), and methodology (approaches to conducting research) (Tracy, 2020). *Interpretivism*, also referred to as naturalism or social constructivism, is the paradigm typically associated with qualitative research, as qualitative researchers are primarily concerned with making sense of participants' interpretations of their lived experiences (Creswell & Poth, 2018). Naturalism assumes the existence of multiple subjective realities; the interdependent relationship between the researcher and the researched; context-specific, non-causal attributions; and value-bound inquiry (Guba & Lincoln, 1982).

Although some arts-based scholars position ABR as a unique research paradigm (Leavy, 2020), others view it as a point on a continuum that spans diverse approaches to qualitative research that range from science to art (Ellingson, 2009). Given that many of the arts-based tenets identified by Leavy (2020) (i.e., evocation, re(presenting), authenticity, truthfulness, aesthetic power, and resonance) overlap with Tracy's (2010) criteria for and practices of excellent qualitative research (i.e., sincerity, transparency, crystallization, resonance, aesthetic, evocative representation), arts-based and interpretivist approaches may share too many underlying assumptions to be categorized as distinct paradigms. I contend that Ellingson's (2009) conceptualization of a qualitative continuum offers a heuristic meta-methodological perspective for arts-based researchers because it offers infinite possibilities for combining science-centered, middle ground, and art-centered approaches within and across nearly all paradigms. Drawing a parallel with Ellingson's (2009) discussion of crystallization, the only paradigm that does not complement ABR is positivism because of its unwavering pursuit of objective, "ahistorical, unbiased, universal truth" (p. 4). Thus, ABR practices are congruent with postpositivist, interpretive, critical, and postmodern/-structural paradigms. From my standpoint, having moved across the continuum during the course of my career, I have identified with postpositivist, interpretive, critical, and postmodern perspectives. Although I locate iconographic research poetry at the artistic end of the continuum, I recognize that its methodology also reflects middle-ground qualitative/interpretive methods and analyses, as I describe in the next section.

2.2 Analysis

The process of generating iconographic research poetry from qualitative data begins during the analytic process. Although there are diverse approaches to analyzing qualitative data, I recommend conducting an iterative thematic analysis (Tracy, 2013, 2020), followed by a metaphor analysis (Tracy et al., 2006). Drawing upon contemporary versions of grounded theory (Charmaz, 2006; Lindlof & Taylor, 2011), Tracy (2013, 2020) described *iterative analysis* or *phronetic iterative analysis* as a cyclical process that alternates between *emic* and *etic coding*. In other words, the researcher sorts data into categories that are derived organically (emic), as well as from existing theory and research (etic).

The first step of the analytic process is to immerse oneself in the data: While transcribing interviews, I revel in the opportunity to spend several hours revisiting each conversation that I had with my interviewees. Although some people may perceive this task to be tedious, I believe it is beneficial to relive these conversations because the process brings scholars closer to their participants. In addition, repeatedly listening to audio recordings allows researchers to become more familiar with participants' speaking style, mannerisms, and colloquialisms (Miller, 2019). Reflecting on one of her research poems, Miller observed: "The speaker's unique voice—her vernacular syntax and colloquialisms (e.g., "I don't do no work'; 'I got me own furniture') evoke a memorable sense of personality" (p. 19). From the perspective of a communication scholar and research poet, this familiarity is important because it enables the researcher to listen carefully to the rhythm and internal rhymes embedded in participants' speech—features that are essential notes in the music of poetry. For example, Ellingson (2011) used stylistic repetition of the words "make sure" several times within one research poem to illustrate how dialysis technicians communicate vigilance.

Once I transcribe an interview, I then email the text to the respondent, who verifies its accuracy. Some researchers would argue that this step is unnecessary, but I believe that this type of *member check* (Ellingson, 2009) is important because it enhances the accuracy of the data by asking respondents to verify that the transcriptions are correct. In addition, it provides an opportunity to ask respondents whether or not they want to use a pseudonym, remove identifiers, edit any statements, or approve any verbatim quotations that will be used in the final paper. During this stage, researchers can also ask participants probes to clarify ambiguous statements. For example, in one research project, I asked a participant to explain whom she meant when she used the referent, "they." I recommend using different colored fonts to indicate which text is original and which text was added during the member checks.

During the primary stage of analysis, qualitative scholars typically engage in *first-level* (Tracy, 2013, 2020), *initial* (Charmaz, 2006), or *open coding* (Lindlof & Taylor, 2011), which are similar to the emic, or organically derived codes described previously. By combing transcripts line by line or sentence by sentence, researchers can describe the content of the data. Although there are a wide variety of approaches to coding, I typically employ a manual approach, using a pencil to underline statements that reflect Owen's (1984) criteria of recurrence, repetition, and forcefulness. Next, scholars can use *edge-coding*, writing notes in the margin to label underlined statements with words that encapsulate the thoughts, feelings, or behaviors that the participants describe. These first-level codes (Tracy, 2013, 2020) are inductively derived and descriptive in nature. For example, in a study that I conducted about single mothers of children with mental illness, I identified ten first-level codes, such as "ex-husband involved" or "ex-husband not involved."

During the next stage of analysis, qualitative researchers usually engage in *second-level* (Tracy, 2013, 2020), *focused* (Charmaz, 2006), or *axial coding* (Lindlof & Taylor, 2011). These types of coding correspond with etic coding, which derives category labels from pre-existing theories or models, as previously discussed. By organizing primary codes into overarching categories, scholars can begin to analyze and interpret the data in terms of their research questions. Researchers can write analytic comments or memos (Charmaz, 2006; Tracy, 2013, 2020) in order to explore how coding categories relate to one another. In addition, by connecting participants' statements to relevant scholarly concepts, they can begin to explore how the data are related to the existing body of research. For example, in my study about single mothers, I identified eight second-level codes, such as "courtesy stigma." I noted that stigma appeared to perpetuate social isolation in single mothers of children with mental illness.

Finally, I recommend conducting a *metaphor analysis*, which involves sifting through the data to identify metaphors that participants use to frame their experience. Poets (e.g., Oliver, 1994), linguists (Lakoff & Johnson, 2003), and researchers (Malvini Redden et al., 2013; Tracy et al., 2006) have identified linguistic markers that typically signal metaphor and simile use, such as "like" and "as." By searching for both explicit and implicit references to metaphors and being mindful of dominant cultural metaphors (e.g., the Western idiom "time is money," described by Lakoff & Johnson, 2003), researchers can identify underlying schemas, or conceptual frameworks, that participants use to make sense of their experience. These root metaphors, then, can provide an alternative lens with which scholars can view their data. For example, Smith and Eisenberg (1987) conducted a classic study of conflict at

Disneyland that revealed how employees and management viewed their organization through two competing metaphors, family and drama, which reflected incompatible worldviews. More recently, Malvini Redden et al. (2013) examined metaphors that people with substance use disorders employed as they engaged in sensemaking about medication-assisted treatment. With respect to poetic inquiry, Prendergast (2012) argued that metaphor is an essential element of method. Metaphor analysis is particularly well suited to creating iconographic research poetry because a metaphor can be easily represented with a visual image.

2.3 Representation

After researchers complete the metaphor analysis, they are ready to begin the process of representation. As Ellingson (2009) offered, "producing artistic representations requires analytical thinking, conscious reflection, and strategic choices concerning which details to include, what the artistic account's purpose and audience are, and what moral or lesson it portrays" (p. 60). My goal as a research poet is to offer the reader an aesthetic and evocative, rather than a solely analytic interpretation of the data. I begin by identifying verbatim quotations from the interview transcriptions that best illustrate the metaphors that I uncovered during my analysis. I heed Ellingson's (2011) advice to choose excerpts that are also aesthetically appealing (i.e., eloquent and compelling), as well as those which reflect embodied experience (Ellingson, 2017; Faulkner, 2018). For example, in a recent study about the experiences of teaching and learning in an arts-based research class (Meyer, 2023), several students used the journey metaphor to describe their experiences conducting research. I selected the following excerpt to represent the journey metaphor because it had compelling, vivid, embodied language:

> It was like climbing small mountains. Each time we would complete a little piece and reach the top of that mountain, we would give each other a pat on the back and then feel a drive to move on to the next one.

Next, I create visual images that represent the metaphors and accompanying verbatim quotations. Two methods that I have employed to create iconographic research poetry (Meyer, 2017) rely on word processing software, such as Microsoft Word: The first technique uses linear lines of typed text; the second embeds text within clip art or icons. A third method uses a graphic design program, such as InDesign, to layer images and text and create new shapes using words from the poem. See Table 2.1 for a comparison of the three methods that can be used to create iconographic research poetry.

Typed text. The first technique that I use to create iconographic research poems employs line breaks to delineate the shape of the word-image. This approach is similar to techniques employed by classic poets such as Kostelanetz (1970) and Swenson (1970), who originally used typewriters to write concrete and iconographic poems. Different elements of typography (i.e., font, format, spacing, capitalization)

Table 2.1 Three methods for creating iconographic research poems

	Typed text	Clip art/icon	Graphic design
Description	Employs line breaks to delineate the shape of the word-image, using a word processing program such as Microsoft Word	Uses Microsoft clip art or icon to create an image behind the text	Utilizes a graphic design program, such as Adobe InDesign, to create layered images and text
Composition	Comprised of linear lines of typed text	Consists of text embedded within clip art or icon	Contains layered images and text

can be applied to emphasize certain words and evoke emotions that are consistent with respondents' words. For example, in my work, I sometimes use all uppercase letters or bold formatting to indicate the forcefulness with which respondents express an idea or emotion. However, Solt (1968) cautioned poets to think carefully about their typographical decisions:

> [. . .] for the form, weight, and scale of letters and words can be used to heighten, can at best become physically part of what he has to say; they can unobtrusively have little effect upon what he has to say; or they can intrude a discordant note into what he has to say. (p. 61)

To create an iconographic poem comprised of typed text, begin by opening a Microsoft Word document. (At the time I wrote this chapter, I was using MS Word 2019, but these instructions can be adapted easily to a different version of the software.) Think of a shape that represents the metaphor you want to depict. For example, you might visualize the shape of a mountain to represent the student who used a mountain climbing metaphor to describe her academic journey. Start at the far left margin and begin typing the text of your poem, comprised of your participants' words. Like Ellingson (2011), Glesne (1997), Miller (2019), and Schoone (2018), I recommend retaining the exact words participants used in an effort to remain true to their voices. In the event that it is necessary to add words for clarification, Glesne recommends enclosing the words in brackets to indicate that the words are yours, rather than the participant's. If a quotation is too long, consider condensing the prose, editing out redundant words and phrases that do not directly support the theme (Ellingson, 2011). Alternatively, when a quotation is not long enough to create a desired word-image, you may decide to weave multiple participants' voices together in one poem by placing them one after the other, separating excerpts with visual cues, such as multiple asterisks or changes in the direction of text.

Using the tab key, space bar, and hard returns, create the shape of a mountain on the page. Note that some shapes will give you more freedom to exercise poetic license than others. Whenever possible, think strategically about line breaks: Not only do you want to create a poem that approximates a given shape, you also want to use long lines to build tension, followed by short lines that signal an abrupt change in direction. Faulkner (2009, 2020) urged research poets to consider how line breaks and enjambment can be employed to transform interview data into found poetry. For example, you might use enjambment (a line break where syntax doesn't naturally pause) to signal a poetic turn. Just as repetition can emphasize a recurring theme in

2.3 Representation

the data, an unexpected break in the metrical contract may represent the voice of an outlier. Add space between words to slow the pace down; remove punctuation to speed up the pace.

Once you have converted your participants' words to an iconographic research poem composed of typed text, you can edit it, using white space, indentation, font size, and line spacing to maximize your use of the page. If you plan to submit your research poetry for publication, you may want to consult the journal's manuscript preparation guidelines. In general, it is a good idea to create camera-ready images that are in .tif or .jpeg format with a resolution of at least 300dpi and no larger than 4.5 inches. Once you have finalized your iconographic research poem, look back at what you have created. (See Fig. 2.1.) If your research poem is more than 40 words, congratulate yourself for resisting the tyranny of the block quotation. In Vannini's (2019) words, "Indentation is lame. It kills quotes. It kills them, and it puts them in a coffin in the middle of the page" (p. 45).

Clip art/icons. An alternative technique that can be employed to generate iconographic research poetry uses Microsoft clip art or icons to create an image behind the text. This practice serves two purposes: First, it can help writers visualize the shape of the iconographic research poem, so they know where to place line breaks in order to create the image. Second, it can provide a lightly shaded background that allows readers to more easily recognize the shape of the iconographic research poem. Although some scholars argue that visual poetry should demand readers to actively engage with the text (Bohn, 2011), I urge researchers to attempt to strike a balance—challenge your readers, but don't produce a word-image that is so difficult to decipher that novice poetry readers give up.

To create an iconographic poem using clip art or icons, begin by opening a document in Microsoft Word. After making a hard return at the top of the page, select "insert online pictures." In the search box, type "clip art" and the word for a shape that represents the metaphor you want to depict. For example, if you were to use the previous mountain climbing metaphor, you would type "mountain." Make sure that the box "Creative Commons only" is checked: If you plan to submit your research poetry for publication, the image you use must be in the public domain and free to use, share and modify, even for commercial purposes. Alternatively, you could select "insert icons" and type "mountain." Select the image, then select "insert" to place

Fig. 2.1 Typed text iconographic research poem: "Mountain"

It
was
like climbing
small mountains.
Each time we would
complete a little piece and
reach the top of that mountain, we
would give each other a pat on the back
and then feel a drive to move on to the next one.

Fig. 2.2 Clipart/icon mountain

it in your document. (See Fig. 2.2.) Under Format, select "Graphics Fill," then a transparent color, such as "White, Background 1, Darker 5%." Adjust the height and width of your image to approximate the size you want your poem to be. Sometimes it helps to type your poem in the shape of a prose poem or paragraph and adjust your margins and line spacing so that you can get a sense of the height and width of your text. Select "position in line with text" and "wrap text behind text."

To start typing your poem, cut and paste the material that you want to fill your image in the line at the top of the document. (See Fig. 2.3.) Next, drag the image so that it is positioned over the text with the first word in the place you want your poem to begin. (See Fig. 2.4.) Adjust the font size and line spacing as needed to match the size of your image and use the tab key and space bar to create white space so that your text fills only the image. (See Fig. 2.5.) Once you have filled the image with text, you can select "White, Background 1" from "Format > Graphics Fill," if you want to remove the background image. You can also select the picture box and delete it without deleting the text of your poem. You can then display your ruler and gridlines, which will allow you to align your text and smooth out any rough edges. However, you may want to resist the temptation to "tuck in" ragged ends if your participants address subject matter that resists coloring inside the lines.

Graphic design. A third technique that can be used to create iconographic research poetry employs a graphic design program, such as Adobe InDesign. (At the time I wrote this chapter, I was using Adobe InDesign 2019, but these instructions can

---

It was like climbing small mountains. Each time we would complete a little piece and reach the top of that mountain, we would give each other a pat on the back and then feel a drive to move onto the next one.

Fig. 2.3 Quotation: "it was like climbing small mountains ..."

2.3 Representation

> It was like climbing small mountains. Each time we would complete a little piece and reach the top of that mountain, we would give each other a pat on the back and then feel a drive to move onto the next one.

Fig. 2.4 Clipart/icon mountain and quotation

Fig. 2.5 Clipart/icon iconographic research poem: "two mountains"

```
                         It
                      was like
                    climbing small
                   mountains. Each time
                  we would complete a
                  little piece and
                  reach the top of that              on to
                  mountain, we would             move      the
                  give each other a pat on         to         next
                  the back and then feel a    drive             one.
```

be adapted easily to a different version of the software.) To generate a poem using InDesign, first open a new blank document by going to File > New > Document. Create a standard 8.5 inch × 11 inch document. In the new document box, change the units from the preset, picas, to inches. Type 8.5 in the width box and 11 in the height box, and then click "Create." If you would prefer a landscape orientation for your poem, click on the landscape icon.

Start your poem by thinking of a shape that represents your underlying metaphor. For example, to create a visual representation of the mountain climbing metaphor, you might choose three triangle-shaped mountains. Click on the Rectangle Tool in the left-hand toolbar and place three rectangles across the bottom of the document. As you place each rectangle, you can adjust the size to make it smaller or larger. Using the drop-down menu at the top of the page, select Object > Convert Shape > Triangle. (See Fig. 2.6.) Next, break the quotation up into three subsections, each one a bit longer than the previous one, to give you the requisite number of words to build three word-mountains, each one larger than the preceding one. (See Fig. 2.7.)

To create a text box within the blank space of each mountain image, click on the Type Tool, a capital T icon in the left-hand toolbar. Place three text boxes on the document, one within each mountain. Fill in each box with the text from the quotation and begin shaping the mountains. Each line should get increasingly longer as the slope of the word-mountain descends. Once each word-mountain is complete, you can add texture to the words by choosing a font and editing the style of the words you want to stand out in the poem. Select a font that matches the emotional tone of the quotation and use all uppercase letters or bold formatting to emphasize important words. Make each mountain a different size by increasing the font size as the mountains get larger, moving from left to right. To increase the size of the font to fit the space, highlight the text and either use the arrows to change the font size one point at a time or type in the size you think would work best. (See Fig. 2.8.)

To complete the scene, you might consider adding background features such as a sun and clouds. To find a clear image of a sun and clouds, conduct an advanced

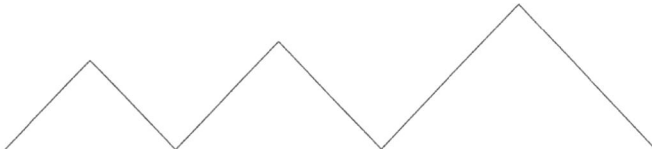

Fig. 2.6 InDesign triangle mountains

It was like climbing small mountains.
Each time we would complete a little piece and reach the top of that mountain,
we would give each other a pat on the back and then feel a drive to move on to the next one.

Fig. 2.7 Quotation in three parts: "it was like climbing small mountains..."

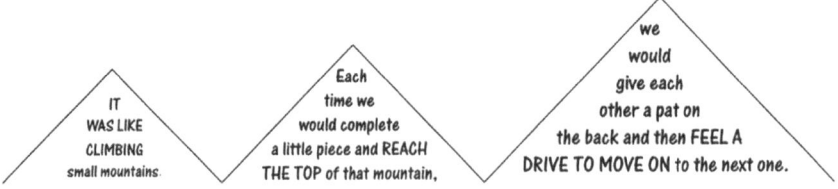

Fig. 2.8 InDesign mountains and quotation

Fig. 2.9 InDesign iconographic research poem: "three mountains"

Google image search for "sun outline" and "cloud outline," and download an image that is large enough that it will not look pixelated or grainy when you resize it in your document. As in the clip art/icon poem, be sure to filter images for usage rights. To place the image, go to File > Place, and InDesign will prompt you to choose an image for your document. Place the sun image in the top left corner of the page by clicking on the screen where you would like the top left corner of your image to start, and then pull the cursor across the page to make the image the desired size. Follow the same steps to place your clouds. Now that you have your mountains placed and your sky arranged, your InDesign iconographic research poem is complete. (See Fig. 2.9.) Praise it with an emphatic, "Summit!"

2.4 Member and Artist-Poet Reflections

Once researchers complete an installation of iconographic research poems that represent their findings, the next step is to solicit *member reflections* (Tracy, 2010) by sharing a draft of their poems with key informants and inviting them to assess the resonance (Tracy, 2010) of the analysis and representation. Creating a space in which to dialogue about research findings with participants enhances the credibility of one's research. I argue that, rather than seeking to validate the accuracy of one's findings, scholars ought to assess the extent to which their work resonates with respondents. In other words, do your findings reverberate with your participants in a meaningful way? Do they identify with the metaphors that you uncovered? Do they find your research poems accessible?

In addition to conducting member reflections, researchers can also solicit feedback from artists and poets. If you don't have any friends who are artists or poets, you might consider joining a local writing group or taking an art class in your community. Alternatively, you could go to a poetry reading or art exhibit and invite a poet or artist whose work resonates with you to collaborate with you. Ask your new writing or artistic partner whether they were moved by your iconographic research poems: Did you achieve aesthetic merit (Tracy, 2010) or artistic concentration (Faulkner, 2009, 2020) by presenting your text in a beautiful, evocative, and artistic way? By incorporating artist-poet feedback, one can improve the aesthetic quality of one's work. In addition, engaging in artist-poet reflection is an opportunity for you to build community with other writers and artists in your area. By sharing your poems with others, you are creating a space for dialogue about poetic inquiry in your culture. Every such conversation about poetry is revolutionary because it liberates poems that might otherwise languish in the drawer.

Finally, scholars can incorporate participant and poet-artist feedback to revise poems that are difficult to read. For example, if the direction of the text in some poems was difficult to discern, research poets can add white space, change line breaks, and use formatting to reduce ambiguity. In these ways, researchers can revise their iconographic research poems to reduce reader burden. Although readers may still need to "perform a series of gyrations in order to arrive at their destination" (Bohn, 2011, p. 16), research poets can facilitate the decoding process by providing visual and verbal cues that "guide the reader through the intersemiotic maze" (Bohn, 2011, p. 16). For example, you can signal the beginning of a poem with a letter that is larger than the rest or set off with bold formatting. If your poem is circular, readers tend to proceed in a clockwise direction. I used both of these techniques when I wrote an iconographic research poem in the form of a juggler to represent the experiences of caregivers of children with mental illness (Meyer, 2017). (See Fig. 2.10.)

2.5 Summary

In this chapter, I have described methods that can be used to create and design iconographic research poetry. Analytic strategies such as iterative thematic analysis and metaphor analysis can be used to generate iconographic research poetry from qualitative data. Word processing software such as Microsoft Word and graphic design programs such as Adobe InDesign can be employed to create iconographic research poetry using techniques that range from typed text, clip art/icons, to layered images and text. By soliciting member reflections, as well as feedback from artists and poets, researchers can assess the resonance of their work and enhance the aesthetic quality of their research poems. In the process, they can create a space to engage in dialogue about poetic inquiry in their communities.

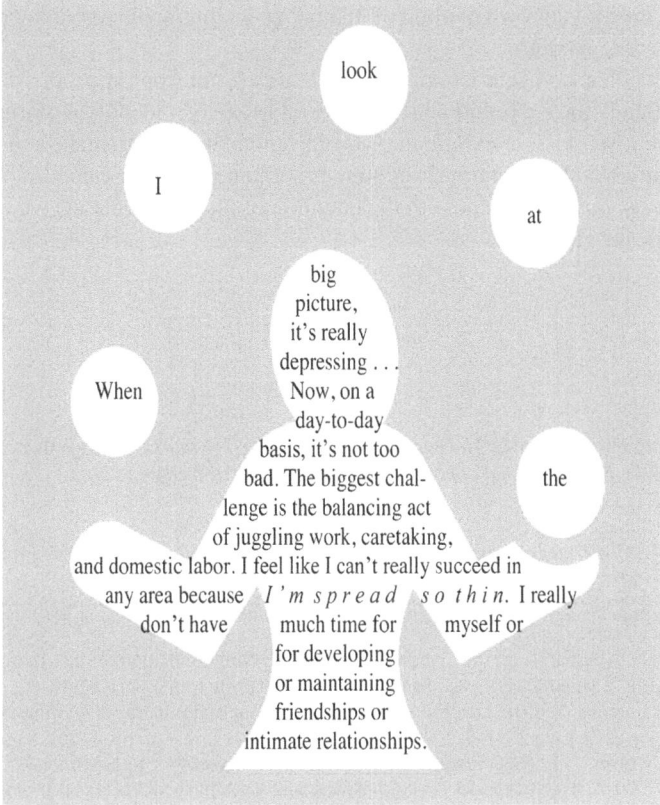

Fig. 2.10 "Juggler." *Source* Meyer (2017). Reprinted by permission of the author. Clipart source https://game-icons.net/1x1/lorc/juggler.html by Lorc. CC BY 3.0

2.6 Exercises

1. Examine a data set from a current or former qualitative research project. Conduct a metaphor analysis by sifting through the interview data and identifying metaphors that participants use to frame their experience. What new insights do these metaphors offer about your participants?
2. Take one of the metaphors that you identified in the previous exercise. Think of some visual images that represent the metaphor. Which visual image do you think fits best? Why?
3. Identify one or more quotations from your data set that evidence the metaphor that you identified in the previous exercise. Use one of the techniques described in this chapter (i.e., typed text, clip art/icons, or graphic design) to create your own iconographic research poem. If you are proficient in the visual arts or graphic

design, invent your own method of making an iconographic research poem with your favorite medium.
4. Solicit feedback on your iconographic research poem from a poet or artist. If you don't already have a friend who is a poet or artist, then identify a writing group, workshop, art class, or exhibit that you can attend in order to make a new friend. Find out when their next meeting time is and put it on your calendar. When the day comes, go to the event with the intention of meeting someone who can help you improve your craft.

References

Baxter, L., & Babbie, E. (2004). *The basics of communication research*. Wadsworth.
Bohn, W. (2011). *Reading visual poetry*. Fairleigh Dickinson University Press.
Butler-Kisber, L. (2010). *Qualitative inquiry: Thematic, narrative and arts-informed perspectives*. Sage.
Charmaz, K. (2006). *Constructing grounded theory: A practical guide through qualitative analysis*. Sage.
Creswell, J., & Poth, C. (2018). *Qualitative inquiry & research design: Choosing among five approaches*. Sage.
Deetz, S. (2001). Alternative perspectives in organizational communication studies. In L. Putnam & F. Jablin (Eds.), *Handbook of organizational communication* (pp. 3–46). Sage.
Denzin, N. & Lincoln, Y. (2018). Introduction: The discipline and practice of qualitative research. In N. Denzin & Y. Lincoln (Eds.), Handbook of qualitative research (pp. 1–26). Sage.
Ellingson, L. (2009). *Engaging crystallization in qualitative research: An introduction*. Sage.
Ellingson, L. (2011). The poetics of professionalism among dialysis technicians. *Health Communication, 26*(1), 1–12. https://doi.org/10.1080/10410236.2011.527617
Ellingson, L. (2017). *Embodiment in qualitative research*. Routledge.
Faulkner, S. (2009). *Poetry as method: Reporting research through verse*. Left Coast Press.
Faulkner, S. (2018). *Real women run: Running as feminist embodiment*. Routledge.
Faulkner, S. (2020). *Poetic inquiry: Craft, method, and practice* (2nd ed.). Routledge.
Frey, L., Botan, C., & Kreps, G. (2000). *Investigating communication: An introduction to research methods* (2nd ed.). Prentice Hall.
Glesne, C. (1997). That rare feeling: Re-presenting research through poetic transcription. *Qualitative Inquiry, 3*(2), 202–221. https://doi.org/10.1177/107780049700300204
Guba, E. G., & Lincoln, Y. S. (1982). Epistemological and methodological bases of naturalistic inquiry. *Educational Communication and Technology, 30*(4), 233–252. https://doi.org/10.1007/BF02765185
Kostelanetz, R. (1970). *Imaged words & worded images*. Outerbridge & Dienstfrey.
Lakoff, G., & Johnson, M. (2003). *Metaphors we live by*. University of Chicago Press.
Leavy, P. (2020). *Method meets art: Arts-based research practice* (3rd ed.). Guilford Press.
Lindlof, T. R., & Taylor, B. C. (2011). *Qualitative communication research methods* (2nd ed.). Sage.
Malvini Redden, M., Tracy, S., & Shafer, M. (2013). Substance abusers' sensemaking of medication-assisted treatment. *Qualitative Research, 23*(7), 951–962. https://doi.org/10.1177/1049732313487802
Meyer, M. (2017). Concrete research poetry: A visual representation of metaphor. *Art/Research International: A Transdisciplinary Journal, 2*(1), 32–57. https://doi.org/10.18432/R2KS6F

References

Meyer, M. (2023). Stepping up, keeping on track, and pulling your own weight: Collaborative arts-based service-learning metaphors. *The Journal of Community Engagement and Higher Education, 15*(2), 19–27.

Miller, E. (2019). Creating research poetry: A nursing home example. In A. Humble & M. Radina (Eds.), *How qualitative data analysis happens: Moving beyond 'themes emerged'* (pp. 18–33). Routledge.

Oliver, M. (1994). *A poetry handbook*. Harcourt.

Owen, W. F. (1984). Interpretive themes in relational communication. *Quarterly Journal of Speech, 70*(3), 274–287. https://doi.org/10.1080/00335638409383697

Poem Generator. (n.d.). https://www.poem-generator.org.uk/

Prendergast, M. (2012). Education and/as art: A found poetry suite. *International Journal of Education & the Arts, 13*(2), 1–18.

Rose, W. (1980). *Lost copper*. Malki Museum.

Schoone, A. (2018). The found poem as a constellation. In P. Sameshima, A. Fidyk, K. James, & C. Leggo (Eds.), *Poetic inquiry: Enchantment of place* (pp. 271–280). Vernon Press.

Smith, M. J. (1988). *Contemporary communication research methods*. Wadsworth.

Smith, R., & Eisenberg, E. (1987). Conflict at Disneyland: A root metaphor analysis. *Communication Monographs, 54*(4), 367–380.

Solt, M. (1968). *Concrete poetry: A world view*. Indiana University Press.

Swenson, M. (1970). *Iconographs*. Charles Scribner's Sons.

Tracy, S. (2010). Qualitative quality: Eight 'big-tent' criteria for excellent qualitative research. *Qualitative Inquiry, 16*(10), 837–851. https://doi.org/10.1177/1077800410383121

Tracy, S. (2013). *Qualitative research methods: Collecting evidence, crafting analysis, communicating impact*. Wiley.

Tracy, S. (2020). *Qualitative research methods: Collecting evidence, crafting analysis, communicating impact* (2nd ed.). Wiley

Tracy, S., Lutgen-Sandvik, P., & Alberts, J. (2006). Nightmares, demons, and slaves: Exploring the painful metaphors of workplace bullying. *Management Communication Quarterly, 20*(2), 148–185. https://doi.org/10.1177/0893318906291980

Vannini, P. (2019). *Doing public ethnography: How to create and disseminate ethnographic and qualitative research to wide audiences*. Routledge.

Open Access This chapter is licensed under the terms of the Creative Commons Attribution 4.0 International License (http://creativecommons.org/licenses/by/4.0/), which permits use, sharing, adaptation, distribution and reproduction in any medium or format, as long as you give appropriate credit to the original author(s) and the source, provide a link to the Creative Commons license and indicate if changes were made.

The images or other third party material in this chapter are included in the chapter's Creative Commons license, unless indicated otherwise in a credit line to the material. If material is not included in the chapter's Creative Commons license and your intended use is not permitted by statutory regulation or exceeds the permitted use, you will need to obtain permission directly from the copyright holder.

Chapter 3
The State of Concrete and Iconographic Research Poetry

Abstract In this chapter, the author reviews recent exemplars of concrete and iconographic research poetry. She traces the development of concrete and iconographic research poetry in journal articles and chapters in edited books, paying attention to the methods that each research poet employed to create their word-images. In addition to describing and interpreting recently published works, the author shares some previously unpublished iconographic ekphrastic research poetry that has promising implications for collaborative arts-based inquiry. She then engages in a reflexive examination of ethical tensions that she experienced as a non-Native scholar writing about Native artists and their works of art during her iconographic ekphrastic project. The author concludes this chapter with some writing exercises designed to encourage readers to open their eyes, ears, and hearts to sources of poetic inspiration from the natural world.

Keywords Arts-based research (ABR) · Arts-based educational research (ABER) · ABR methods · Concrete research poetry · Ekphrastic research poetry · Ethics · Iconographic research poetry · Reflexivity · Research poetry

In this chapter, I review recent exemplars of concrete and iconographic research poetry. Beginning with my 2017 publication in *Art/Research International*, I trace the development of concrete and iconographic research poetry in journal articles and chapters in edited books (e.g., Lahman & DeOliveira, 2021; Lahman et al., 2019; Miller, 2019; Penwarden & Schoone, 2021; Schoone, 2018, 2019, 2020). Although I made the distinction between different types of concrete poems in my introductory chapter and choose to use the term "iconographic" to refer to my own work, I will use the terms that the authors employed to describe their poetry here because I want to validate the authors' portrayals of their own works. In my review, I pay attention to the methods that each research poet employed to create their word-images. In addition to describing and interpreting recently published works, I share some previously unpublished iconographic ekphrastic research poetry that has promising implications for collaborative arts-based inquiry. After engaging in a reflexive examination of the ethical tensions that I experienced during my iconographic ekphrastic project, I conclude this chapter with some writing exercises designed to encourage readers to open their eyes, ears, and hearts to sources of poetic inspiration that surround us in the natural world.

3.1 From Casserole to Constellation: A Review of Concrete and Iconographic Research Poetry

In 2017, I published a study about the experiences of caregivers of children with mental illness (Meyer, 2017). In this paper, I used autoethnographic and ethnographic methods to explore the experiences of eight single mothers of children and young adults with mental illness. I employed the methods described in Chap. 2 to conduct a metaphor analysis of semi-structured interview data. Next, I generated an installation of iconographic research poems to represent metaphors that emerged from the data (e.g., the rollercoaster poem featured in Chap. 1). In addition, I created iconographic poems to represent themes in the scholarly literature about parenting children with mental illness. For example, I employed the shape of a casserole to represent the stigma experienced by caregivers of children with mental illness. (See "Casserole" in Fig. 3.1.) This typed text poem is shaped like a casserole to represent the different levels of social support received by parents of a child with a physical illness and parents of a child with mental illness. In this research project, I made a significant contribution to the existing body of research poetry by representing my literature review and research findings with iconographic research poems, a novel form of poetic inquiry.

<u>Do you know</u>

<u>the difference between being a mother of a child with mental illness and a</u>

mother of a child with a broken leg? I know it sounds like a joke, but it's

not. Please don't laugh when I say, "casserole," because it's not funny.

When your child breaks a leg, the church organizes a brigade of casserole-

makers: Friends, family, neighbors, co-workers bring food. But when your

child is in the psych ward, there are no casseroles. Alone, you set an empty

place for stigma at the table. Do not blame the church, the neighborhood

association, or the social committee at work: It's not their fault—you

didn't tell them. Don't blame yourself, either: Blame it on stigma.

<u>Invite them over for a stigma casserole.</u>

Fig. 3.1 Iconographic research poem: "Casserole." *Source* Meyer (2017). Reprinted by permission of the author

In 2018, Schoone wrote a book chapter based on his 2015 dissertation research about the lived experiences of tutors in alternative education in New Zealand. In 2020, Schoone published an extended treatment of his dissertation research project in a book monograph. His study employed concrete poetry to create two- and three-dimensional representations of his participants' voices. Schoone presented a clear and detailed description of the process by which he created found poems from interview transcripts, then converted the poems into three-dimensional constellations comprised of polystyrene balls, labeled with words and phrases, and suspended against the night sky with nylon string. Schoone photographed the constellations, then edited the photographs on his computer to enhance the legibility of the text. Influenced by Gomringer, who conceptualized concrete poetry as constellations of words (Gomringer, 1968), and James's (2009) description of *literary cut-ups,* which create new texts from decontextualized fragments, Schoone transformed his data into a unique three-dimensional form of concrete research poetry, exemplified by the poem "Epiphany." (See Fig. 3.2.)

In 2019,Schoone published a book review in the form of a visual poem. Specifically, he created a found poem, using words and phrases from Pappne Demecs and Miller's (2019) participatory research study about tapestry weaving in an aged care facility. Schoone created a visual representation of woven fabric, in which he placed words and phrases from Pappne Demecs and Miller's article. (See "The Loom" in Fig. 3.3.) Because his poem was created in part as a response to visual images of tapestry weaving in the article, his research poem can also be characterized as *ekphrastic poetry*, which Gulla (2018) defined as "a poem written in response to a work of art" (p. 23).

Evonne Miller authored a book chapter about research poetry in 2019. She created a series of research poems from interviews that she conducted with residents in a nursing home in Australia. One of those poems, entitled, "When Your Time Is Up," is a concrete research poem. (See Fig. 3.4.) In this poem, Miller placed her found poetry in the shape of an hourglass to represent how quickly time passes for nursing home residents. Although she doesn't describe the method that she used to create her concrete poem, she appears to have inserted shapes and textboxes into a Microsoft Word document. This poem is powerful because the hourglass image reinforces the idea of time passing quickly for elderly people who are literally and figuratively close to death. The words "When Your Time Is Up" are formatted in bold letters in the title, as well as at the end of the poem, to indicate the pervasiveness of death in her respondents' lived experiences.

Also in 2019, Lahman et al. coauthored an article that used research poetry to represent experiences that the authors had with their Institutional Review Boards (IRBs). One of the poems, written by Maria Lahman, employed concrete research poetry to represent her frustration with the IRB review process surrounding vulnerable populations. (See Fig. 3.5.) The poem, shaped like the letters "I," "R," and "B," is filled with emotion-laden words such as "frustrated," "angry," "blame the messenger," and ends with the words, "BENEFICENCE," "RESPECT," and "JUSTICE" in all uppercase letters, a clarion call to remember the principles on which the Belmont Report was founded. Although Lahman didn't describe the method that she

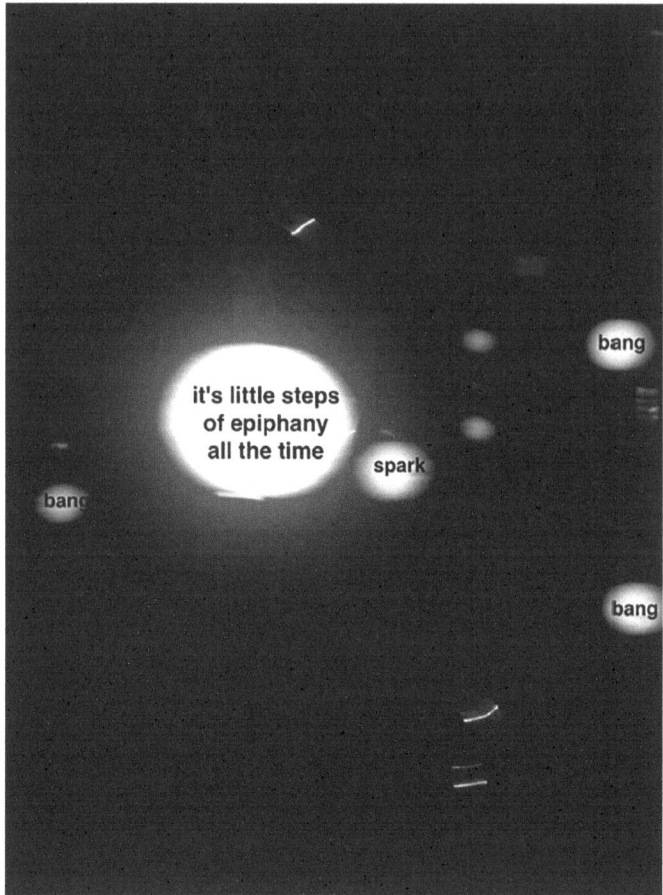

Fig. 3.2 Three-dimensional concrete research poem: "Epiphany." *Source* Schoone (2020). Reprinted by permission

used to create her concrete poem, she appears to have used typed text, tabs, spaces, and hard returns to create the outline of the letters "I," "R," and "B."

More recently, Lahman and DeOliveira (2021) wrote an article that features three-dimensional concrete research poems. Their poems, shaped like flowers and spheres, were found poems derived from handwritten or computer-printed lines of interview transcripts and researchers' reflections. Lahman and DeOliveira provided instructors with a list of needed materials and step-by-step directions for this class activity that used crafting to enable students to hold their data in the palm of their hands. This exercise affords students a unique embodied perspective from which to contemplate their experiences with narrative inquiry.

3.1 From Casserole to Constellation: A Review of Concrete … 43

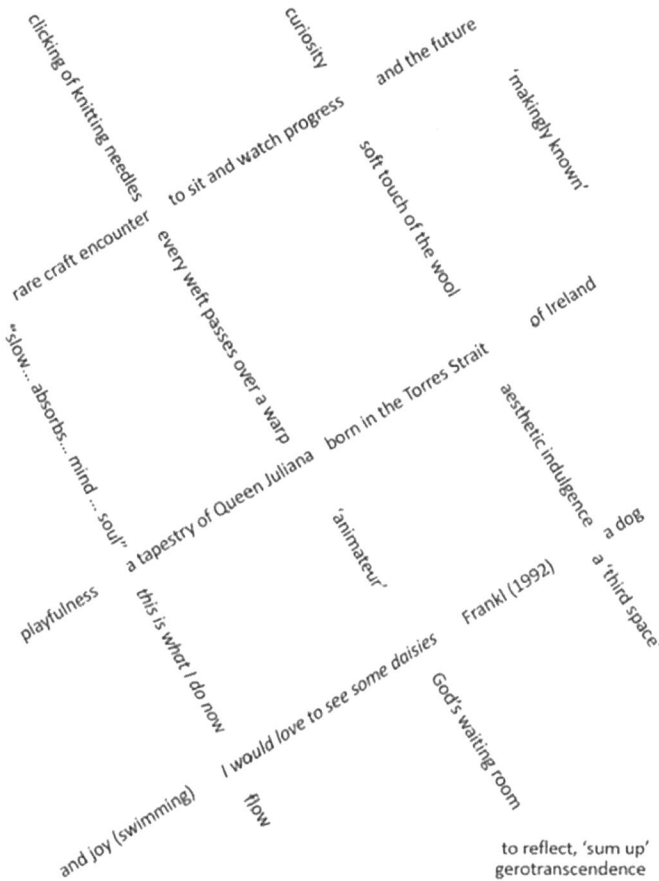

Fig. 3.3 Concrete ekphrastic research poem: "The Loom." *Source* Schoone (2019). Reprinted by permission

Also in 2021, Penwarden and Schoone published an essay and found poetry they created from notes they had taken while listening to presentations at the Fifth International Symposium on Poetic Inquiry. Sarah Penwarden's poem, "The Call" is a concrete poem shaped like the ebb and flow of the sea. Citing Butler-Kisber, Penwarden noted that this poem is also a cluster poem because it "shows different speakers' utterances gathered under one theme" (p. 355). In the endnotes, she linked each line in the poem to a presenter at the symposium to bring transparency to the process of appropriating others' words. In their reflections on their own and one another's poems, the authors raised important questions regarding the ethics of repurposing others' words in found poetry.

Despite the paucity of the existing body of concrete and iconographic research poetry, scholars from around the globe have published their work in scholarly journals and edited books. With techniques that range from typed text to three-dimensional

Fig. 3.4 Concrete research poem: "When Your Time Is Up." *Source* Miller (2019). Reprinted by permission

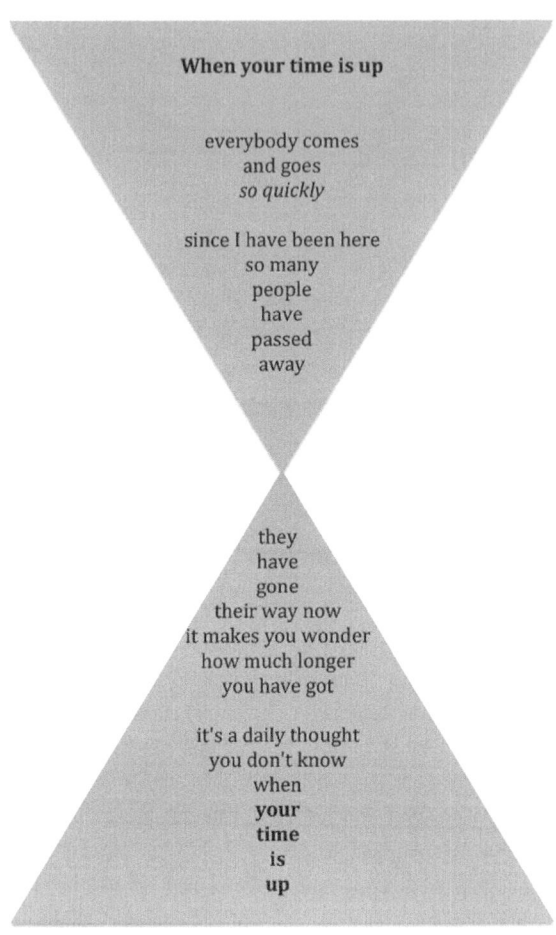

```
I want to believe              I am part of the              solution, but I
get so frustrated              I feel I am on                ly fooling myself.
    I told                     a new professor               the other day that
    I used                     to          be                so          angry
    at the                     w           ay                I           was
    used,                      bl          ame               the messenger, no
    thanks                     for the hard work.            Then it occurred to me
    to use                     all of my knowledge           to publish. A platform
    from                       which    to                   h              elp
    create                     chan     ge.                  T              he
    vulner                     able     are                  a              lso
    power                      ful.     Ethics               are culturally situated.
    Research                   ers      should               be culturally responsive.
    Beware                     eth      ical                 colonistic imperialism.
BENEFICENCE                    RES            PECT           JUSTICE
```

Fig. 3.5 Concrete research poem: "IRB." *Source* Lahman et al. (2019). Reprinted by permission

word-art, concrete and iconographic research poets employ their craft to give voice to their own and their participants' experiences across a variety of contexts, including families with mental illness, nursing home residents, alternative education tutors, institutional review boards, research projects, and research symposia. Most of these scholarly works focus on understanding and representing the lived experiences of people who are members of marginalized groups. Not all of the scholars who create concrete research poetry explicate their method, but those who do describe the process in depth. As Butler-Kisber (2010) observed, "What remains elusive in poetic inquiry, as with any kind of creative process, is the ability to really demonstrate how the poet moves from thoughts, images, and sensations, to the actual shaping of the words on the page" (p. 95). By describing our methodological processes clearly, first generation concrete and iconographic research poets can offer a roadmap for future scholars who want to explore this novel form of poetic inquiry.

3.2 Iconographic Ekphrastic Poetic Inquiry

In addition to the innovative examples noted above, I would like to share some of my unpublished poems that exemplify what I refer to as iconographic ekphrastic poetic inquiry. Although my poems and Schoone's (2019) ekphrastic visual poem share some resemblance in terms of their form, they function much differently. All of our poems use iconographs to respond to artwork; however, Schoone's poem functions as a review of a journal article, whereas my poems convey contextual information about the artists and their relationships. Recall that poetic inquiry differs from research poetry in that it embraces writing as a method of inquiry rather than an alternative means to represent research findings. Akin to Richardson and Walsh (2018), I hope to offer readers a variety of writing practices that will be "restorative... and potentially useful for other artist-teacher-researchers" (p. 161).

I created my first iconographic ekphrastic poem in response to a collaborative ekphrastic project that took place in my community. Before I even knew what ekphrasis was, I was fascinated by collaborative projects that involved art and poetry. In 2016, I was inspired by a call for poems and artwork related to a community arts festival sponsored by the National Alliance on Mental Illness (NAMI) Delaware County, Indiana and the Minnetrista Cultural Center. The exhibit, "Through an Open Window the Light Shines," aimed to combat stigma by showcasing art and poetry by people affected by mental illness. I contacted one of my favorite artists, Christa Barnell, to ask if she would be interested in collaborating on an ekphrastic project with me.

The project originated in a poem that I had originally written as part of an autoethnographic research project about the experience of being a single parent of a child with mental illness. I was delighted when Christa agreed to collaborate with me and overjoyed when Christa invited her mother, Ann, to help her create a painting in response to my research poem. Christa and Ann used images embedded in my poem to paint a visual representation of the angel that I described in my poem.

Fig. 3.6 Painting: "Grounds for a Miracle." *Source* Barnell & Barnell (2016). Reprinted by permission

As you can see, their painting, depicted in Fig. 3.6, is rich with vibrant colors and religious symbolism, including a full-figured angel and a votive depicting the Virgin of Guadelupe.

Ann and I exhibited our poetry and painting at the arts festival. In donating profits from the sale of our poetry and artwork to NAMI, Christa, Ann, and I invested in our community's mental health resources. By disseminating our poetry and art in the community, we created and strengthened connections with other poets, artists, and members of the mental health community. In addition, we made a substantive contribution to the dialogue about mental health in our community.

As I reflected back on the relationship that I developed with Christa and Ann, I felt extremely grateful to have had the opportunity to collaborate with them. I decided to write an iconographic poem to describe the story of our ekphrastic collaboration. I began by creating a washed-out digital image of the painting. Although I gave up the vibrant colors in the original painting, I gained a neutral palette on which I could display text. Next, I compiled all of the archived emails related to this project that Christa, Ann, and I had exchanged over time. I then created a pastiche of emails that I cut and pasted behind the angel. This image, displayed in Fig. 3.7, is a visual representation of our collaborative relationship. Our words literally constitute the background on which the angel rests.

3.2 Iconographic Ekphrastic Poetic Inquiry

FW: NAMI Art Fest
02.15.2016
Hi, Christa! Saw this and thought of you. Any chance you'd be interested in collaborating? marcy

02.18.2016
I've attached two things I'm   thinking of submitting. You may remember the
first, which I shared w/ you   and your mom a few years ago . . .

02.29.2016
Thanks for the affirming reply and   for offering to share my poems w/
your mom. Maybe she will want to   collaborate with me? Oh, happy day! :)

04.16.2016
Hi, I turned it in   yesterday
also with your   poem &
our bio. I say   our bio
because   Christa & I
did a collaboration.   I painted the
candle, background,   child, & she
did the angel & large   coffee cup.
hope you will like it.   Ann
04.18.2016
Thanks for   the update,
Ann. I love   what you and
Christa   created
together! Thank you so   much for sharing
your gifts with me!!
09.11.2016
Thanks for thinking of us to   make visual your poem.
So happy that it will be shared   again in Montreal.
09.12.2016
Hi, Christa! Just a note to say thank you from the   bottom of my heart for
collaborating with me on "grounds for a miracle."   I wish that you could have been
at the opening to see how your painting was displayed: front and center when you walked in the room,
it absolutely popped out of the frame. It was impossible not to be drawn to it: the space right in front of
it was the most crowded place in the room. All evening, I heard people commenting that it was their
favorite work of art. I'm sure your mom told you that it was the first thing that sold, as well. I cannot
thank you enough for donating your creative work to NAMI!

Fig. 3.7 Iconographic ekphrastic poem: "Grounds for a Miracle Backstory"

The iconographic ekphrastic poem in Fig. 3.7 could be characterized as archival poetry (Lahman & Richard, 2014), as well as email poetry (Faulkner & Ruby, 2015; Lahman, 2019). In addition, it is an autobiographical poem, as I am writing about my experience collaborating with the artists. This poem is interesting in that it demonstrates that ekphrasis can be an open-ended process. Ekphrasis can refer not only to a single poem written in response to a work of art (or a single work of art created in response to a poem), but also to a series of artistic and literary representations created in response to one another. Each iteration of the sequence could reveal another layer of the artists' and poets' interpretations of each other's creative works, their experiences creating artistic and literary artifacts, the nature of their relationships, etc. In theory, this process could unfold indefinitely, like an arts-based infinity mirror. Modeling Richardson and Walsh (2018), artists and poets could exchange poetry and artwork in an ongoing collaborative and contemplative process designed to create "conscious and articulate experiences with a healing intent" (p. 162). Over time, collaborative ekphrastic poetry exchanges such as this promote generative learning, as well as authentic relationships (Sameshima & Wiebe, 2018). As Apol (2021) observed, this human, relational aspect of poetic inquiry or "withness" demands relational accountability. Writing this poem allowed me to reflect on and express gratitude for my collaborative relationship with Christa and Ann. In addition, this writing experiment enabled me to understand ekphrasis as an ongoing, reciprocal process. I invite readers to consider how they might employ ekphrasis to cultivate contemplation and gratitude in their own collaborative relationships.

My next three poems were inspired by the 2019 International Symposium on Poetic Inquiry's call for papers. Because the United Nations designated 2019 as the International Year of Indigenous Languages, the symposium's theme was poetry related to indigenous languages. In response to that call, I embarked on an iconographic ekphrastic journey. Moved by Native American art exhibited at the 2018 Eiteljorg Museum Indian Market and Festival, I decided to generate iconographic poems based on works of art that I found to be particularly evocative. This journey was one that changed my poetic voice in unexpected ways.

My first poem is entitled "Four Crows Spy Four Ravens." (See Fig. 3.8.) This poem combines autobiographical and mystical elements. It describes an encounter that I had with some crows in my neighborhood while wearing a t-shirt emblazoned with Gordon Coons' *Four Ravens* 2017 oil on canvas. (See Fig. 3.9.) Although I understand that the guard crow may have just been calling out a warning to alert his friends to the presence of an intruder, in that moment, I felt that the crows called out to me because they recognized the image of the ravens on my shirt. The iconographic poem, shaped like a crow, tells the story of that encounter. Writing the poem allowed me to learn about Coons' art, the nature and language of ravens and crows, and to appreciate the magic that exists in everyday moments in the natural world. Coon's art reflects his Ojibwa and Ottawa heritage, in which ravens and crows are thought to be messengers that mediate communication between humans and the spiritual realm. When the crows called out to me, I understood the crow's messenger role in a new, entirely intuitive way. In writing a poem about this experience, I affirm indigenous and mystical ways of knowing. When I shared my poem with Coons, he validated my work by saying, "Beautiful poem. Your words add more stories to our relatives the crow. Your poem is a joy to read, thank you!" I invite readers to slow down, to listen to indigenous wisdom, and to allow themselves to see the magic that is all around us. The more we slow down and pay attention to the natural and spiritual worlds, the more we allow ourselves to see.

My second poem is entitled "The Gourd Dancers." (See Fig. 3.10.) As I have described elsewhere (Meyer, 2023), this poem was inspired by one of Patria Smith's

3.2 Iconographic Ekphrastic Poetic Inquiry

                  On my chest
             perch four midnight ravens
             with thunderbird hearts,
          their iguana wings and
         canary breasts encircled
        by a black wire that
      ignites four globes of
      light: white shines north-
     west; yellow glows north-
    northeast; red burns southeast;
    black casts shadows southwest.

Three days after the summer solstice, I bike
home from a conversation about poetry and death.
As I cut through the Northside Middle School
parking lot, I hear a guard call out, "Caw! Caw!"

        Out on the Little League field, I see four hunters
        hopping and gliding between the dugout roof and
        the aluminum bleachers behind home plate. Are they
        searching for sunflower seeds dropped by fans at last
        night's game or foil-paper-gum-wrapper-bling to re-
        decorate their nests in the big old Douglas fir across the street?

                          Obsidian wing feathers
                tinted indigo in the evening light, heads cocked to admire
            my t- shirt, they pause to watch me pass with my constable
                              of ravens guarding
                                one heart, two shiny
                                  chrome rims, and
                                  a constellation
                          of spokes.

                                      "Caw! Caw!"
                                          I call in
                                              reply.

Fig. 3.8 Iconographic ekphrastic poem: "Four Crows Spy Four Ravens"

painted gourds, which depicts women at the Copan Powwow. When I met Smith at the Eiteljorg Indian Market, she told me the story behind the gourd painting. Later, I found an archived interview in which Smith tells the story that inspired her painting (DeVinney, 2008a). I transcribed her story verbatim and created an iconographic poem shaped like a gourd with Smith's words. As I transcribed her story, I immersed myself in Smith's lived experience, attending to her accent and the rhythm of her speech. In crafting this poem, I have inscribed a visual image that reflects the shape of Smith's gourd painting with the artist's narrative, which provides context for her artwork. By using Smith's actual words, I have created a found poem that allows the reader to vicariously experience the event that inspired her gourd painting. The iconographic poem is a visual representation of how her Miami heritage and life experience have shaped her artwork. This poem celebrates the Native American powwow as a ceremony that preserves traditional Native American culture, nurtures relationships through community, and offers opportunities for artistic inspiration. Creating the poem allowed me to learn about Smith's art, the cultural significance

Fig. 3.9 Painting: "Four Ravens." *Source* "Gordon Coons, Ojibwa, Four Ravens (2017)." Reprinted by permission

of the powwow, especially the gourd dance, and to appreciate the inspiration for artwork that exists in indigenous cultural ceremonies and Native American women's friendships. In addition, this process enabled me to recognize that archives are a rich source for found poetry: Although I have used interview transcripts to create found poetry and iconographic research poetry before, this is the first time that I have combed archival data for material. This approach is similar to that employed by Lahman and Richard (2014), who used the terms "archival poetry" and "artifact poetry" to refer to research poems created from a body of existing empirical materials (as opposed to found poems generated from data gathered by the researcher). I invite readers to consider which indigenous cultural ceremonies and sources of archival data might inspire their poetic inquiry. The more we quiet our minds and take time to listen to the rhythm of the powwow drummers and voices of wise women and men, the more we allow ourselves to hear.

My third poem is entitled "Turtle Necklace." (See Fig. 3.11.) This poem was inspired by one of Katrina Mitten's lace agate turtle necklaces. Katrina Mitten is the friend that Patria Smith mentions in her story about the gourd dancers at the Copan Powwow. This iconographic poem is shaped like one of Mitten's beaded lace agate turtle necklaces. I used a similar process to create the poem: I found an archived interview in which Mitten talks about the cultural significance of turtles in her work (DeVinney, 2008b). I transcribed her interview and filled an iconographic poem shaped like a turtle with Mitten's words. Toward the bottom of the poem, the words "Miami woman keeps beadworking tradition alive" that fill the turtle's

3.2 Iconographic Ekphrastic Poetic Inquiry   51

> My friend and I—
> my friend, Katrina,
> and I— we used to go
> to the Copan Powwow.
> It's Copan, Oklahoma. It's
> the Delaware Powwow. And it's
> been goin' on for, I think, 100 years or
> more than 100 years. But it's out in the middle
> of nowhere. It's on old man Fall-Leaf's farm. It's by
> a couple of Indian towns. So when you go through the
> towns to get there, it's all closed up, you know, for a few days.
> You can't get a restaurant or anything. Nothin's open because every-
> body's out at Fall-Leaf's farm for Powwow for, I think, a good four days
> anyway. And they'd been camping out there all this time and like, the camp-
> sites then on the farm are inherited then down through the family all this 100 years,
> you know. And so we became friends with a lot of Delaware people. We have a lot of
> friends with the Delaware People and when we arrived there one day, the emcee—he—
> actually he's a Comanche, but we know him—he's married to a Delaware woman—and
> he asked us to come on out in the arena. They were doing a Gourd Dance. In the Gourd
> Dance, it honors veterans—all the men who have fallen in all the wars. The men do the
> dancing—it's not a big dance with a lot of steps—and the women dance behind them, in
> place. They don't move—they don't move their feet. The native women who were dan-
> cing—if you look at some of the women dancers, ekspecially the older ones, their feet
> don't leave the ground. So all the women had their shawls on and Katrina and I grabbed
> our shawls and there were so many of 'em out there that we formed a second line and
> we were behind all those women and some of them had on shawls that represented
> their fallen sons from Vietnam or maybe sons who had served in other wars. And
> other ones, their shawls represented maybe their clan or an organization, you
> know, a quilting place that they belonged to—something special, specific
> to them or their family or their tribe. And so I was behind them, looking
> at all those shawls, and they were so different—every one of them
> was different and they were so beautiful and I thought,
> *what a wonderful painting it would be.*
> I never got around
> to doing the painting,
> so I decided to put it
> on the gourd . . .

Fig. 3.10 Iconographic ekphrastic archival poem: "The Gourd Dancers." *Source* Meyer (2023). Reprinted by permission of the author

legs and necklace's beaded fringe are reminiscent of the title of a newspaper article about Mitten (Gray, 2016). In crafting this poem, I have inscribed a visual image that reflects the shape of Mitten's necklace with the text of her interview, which provides insight about the influence of her Miami and Turtle Clan heritage on her artwork. By using Mitten's own words, I have created an archival poem that allows the reader to appreciate the cultural significance of symbols that she employs in her beadwork. The iconographic poem is a visual representation of how her Miami heritage has shaped her artwork and a way to honor the important contributions that Mitten's embroidery-style native beadwork has made to the preservation of Miami art and culture. Creating the poem allowed me to learn about Mitten's beadwork, the symbolic significance of the turtle, and to appreciate the sources of inspiration for her artwork that stem from her Miami heritage and the natural world. I invite

Fig. 3.11 Iconographic ekphrastic archival poem: Turtle Necklace

```
                            T
              ^             h              ^
              wood-         e              land
              designs    are definitely    things
              v          from nature and what   v
                         we see. So, I do use a lot

                         of things from nature, using

                         the turtle, which I'm—Turtle
                         Clan is my family—so I
                         use a lot of turtles.
                                    vv
                         Miami      v     Woman
                         keeps            bead-
                            w    t    a
                            o    r    l
                            r    a    i
                            k    d    v
                            i    i    e
                            n    t    !
                            g    i    !
                                 o
                                 n
```

readers to think about how their heritage and relationship with the natural world might inspire their poetic inquiry. The more we open our hearts and minds to our sisters and brothers in the natural world, the more we allow ourselves to feel.

3.3 Reflexive Analysis

In the introduction to this book, I noted that reflexivity is a criterion used to evaluate the quality of research poetry (Richardson, 2000). Reflexivity (sometimes referred to as self-reflexivity) is also a hallmark of excellent qualitative research, as it is an indicator of sincerity, integrity, credibility, and trustworthiness (de Souza, 2019; Tracy, 2013, 2020). However, as Olmos-Vega et al. (2023) noted, reflexivity is often overlooked or treated superficially in the research process. In addition, it is often conflated with reflection (Gouzouasis, in press). In the following section, I identify and define three types of reflexivity that pertain to my iconographic ekphrastic poetry

3.3 Reflexive Analysis

project. By engaging in a reflexive examination of the permissions processes related to reprinting the artwork that inspired my poems, I explore ethical tensions that I experienced as a non-Native scholar writing about Native artists and their works of art.

Reflexivity has been conceptualized in various ways. Simply put, *reflexivity* is "thoughtful, conscious self-awareness" (Finlay, 2002, p. 532). Given that a researcher's social positioning inevitably influences their interpretation of data, as well as the research process, scholars are obligated to consider how their presence may have impacted their practices and findings. Reflexivity can be a relational phenomenon, as well. When scholars interact with others during the research process, they have an obligation to engage in *relational reflexivity* (Simon, 2013). Simon observed that when we attend to our inner dialogue and share it with research participants in our outer dialogue, we create opportunities for transparency, authentic communication, and meaningful collaboration. As "qualitative research has been deeply implicated in colonial, racial, and nationalist projects with the relationship between researcher and the 'researched' often mirroring the relationship between oppressors and oppressed" (de Souza, 2019, p. 2), reflexivity also requires that we consider how power dynamics may affect the relationships between researchers and participants. Thus, *intersectional reflexivity* requires that scholars "acknowledge and critique their own intersecting identities, and the privilege and disadvantage they represent in specific contexts" (Ruiz Castro, 2021, p. 217).

Leavy (2020) also argued that arts-based researchers ought to consider power when engaging in reflexivity. Research poets can challenge colonizing discourse by creating poetry based on the experiences of marginalized populations (Sjollema & Yuen, 2018); however, we have a responsibility to honor the individuals whose art or voices are present in our poems by obtaining permission, seeking feedback, and incorporating their suggestions whenever possible. By practicing relational and intersectional reflexivity, we can engage in decolonizing poetic inquiry that upholds high ethical standards. As Apol (2021) revealed, this can be a messy and complicated process at times, particularly when research poets are dominant group members writing about non-dominant group members.

As I examine my experiences related to writing iconographic ekphrastic archival poetry about Native American art, I realize the importance of being transparent about ethical tensions that I experienced during the process of requesting permission to reprint the artist's works of art. At the beginning of this project, I had hoped to juxtapose each of the three poems with photos of the original works of art that had inspired them. However, I was unable to secure permission from Patria Smith or Katrina Mitten: I was unable to locate Smith in person or online; Mitten did not reply to requests that I made in person or over email. Although Coons granted me permission to reprint *Four Ravens*, he initially expressed reluctance to signing the contract my publisher required. As I considered the power relations embedded in my request, I realized there was a long legacy of European Americans asking Native Americans to sign contracts in the United States. In light of this colonizing history, I asked my editor for an exception to the standard procedure. Fortunately, she understood the oppressive power dynamics being reproduced in the situation and agreed to modify the permissions process for Coons. As a way of giving back to the

Native communities with which Coons is affiliated, she also agreed to donate copies of the book to the Heard Museum and the Sequoia Research Center.

Although I was unable to reprint Smith's or Mitten's artwork, I was able to quote material from their archived interviews in my poems because the information was available to the public. Still, I weighed the ethical implications of incorporating their words in my poems without their explicit permission. Was I guilty of cultural appropriation (Rogers, 2006)? Was I violating the principle of "withness" (Apol, 2021) in the relationships that I formed with artists during my poetic inquiry? One thing I knew for sure was that I didn't want to be another "White poet who would be Indian" (Rose, 1980).

As I have described elsewhere (Meyer, 2023) I consulted Jock's (1996) suggestions for non-Native scholars who study Native communities, US copyright fair use factors (APA, 2020), and UNESCO's (1989) recommendations of the safeguarding of traditional culture and folklore. Following UNESCO's directive to "recognize the responsibility of archives to monitor the use made of the materials gathered" (p. 242), I contacted the director of the archive, who granted me permission to quote material from the archived interviews. Although I believe that my decision to incorporate Smith's and Mitten's words was ethical, I recognize that the relationships that I established with them were not as strong as those that I cultivated with the Barnells and Coons. I feel that stronger relationships produced superior outcomes not only in terms of the aesthetic quality of the poems juxtaposed with artwork, but also in terms of being able to give back to the artists in a meaningful way by donating books to their communities.

In conclusion, these four iconographic ekphrastic poems contain autobiographical, archival, and mystical elements that provide additional insight about the original works of art, the artists, and their relationships (with me or with one another). As Gulla (2018) observed, "Often the subject of an ekphrastic poem is not the work of art itself, but the encounter with the work of art that transforms the poet" (p. 23). This writing experiment has changed my poetic voice, allowing me to express gratitude for collaborative relationships, to reconceptualize ekphrasis, to present archival data as found poetry, and to honor indigenous and mystical ways of knowing. I have also gained a deeper appreciation for the power dynamics and ethical issues that non-Native scholars may encounter when requesting permission to use Native scholars' artwork and stories in poetic inquiry. I hope that, in sharing my experiences, I will encourage others to explore the ethical practice of iconographic ekphrastic poetic inquiry. In offering you the following exercises, I invite you to open your eyes, ears, and heart to the wisdom of indigenous ways of knowing and the beauty and magic that surround us in the natural world. Toward these ends, I recommend practicing Cameron's (1992) morning pages and artist dates; Smith's (n.d.) walking meditation; Davis's (2008) yoga poetry; and iconographic ekphrastic poetry in order to cultivate creativity, mindfulness, and embodiment. I suggest that qualitative researchers who are interested in learning more about how to incorporate reflexivity in their research practices read Olmos-Vega et al.'s (2023) "Practical Guide to Reflexivity in Qualitative Research." In addition, I urge non-Native scholars who study Native communities to consult Jocks (1996) and UNESCO's (1989) recommendations on the safeguarding of traditional culture and folklore.

3.4 Exercises

1. Julia Cameron (1992) encouraged writers to engage in two practices: writing morning pages every day and going on an artist date once a week. Morning pages involve writing three unedited pages about absolutely anything every day. Done first thing in the morning, morning pages allow us to turn off our inner censor and de-clutter our minds so that we can free up space for creative thought. Artist dates are excursions that we take by ourselves to places that nurture our creative inner child. A long walk in the woods or a visit to a favorite museum can fill up our inner well of creativity. For the next 30 days, make a commitment to incorporating these practices in your life. How do these activities change your poetic voice?
2. In the previous exercise, if you chose to walk in the woods for your first artist date, you might also enjoy practicing walking meditation. Walking meditation invites us to become more aware of the movement of each step (Smith, n.d.). Most people walk every day, but we typically don't think about how we do it. Walking meditation is a way that we can repurpose an everyday activity as a meditative practice to increase mindfulness. Because walking meditation enhances mindfulness, it quiets the incessant chatter of our minds, which creates a space in which we can gain access to our intuition and creativity. When we practice walking meditation, we literally take steps toward becoming more creative people. For the next 30 days, make a daily commitment to practicing walking meditation. How does this practice change your poetic voice?
3. If you chose to visit a museum for your first artist date in Exercise 1, you might also enjoy practicing iconographic ekphrastic poetic inquiry. Find a work of art that moves you. Ask yourself why it resonates with you. Are there images or symbols in the artwork that are meaningful to you? Are there things that you don't understand? Imagine that the artist invites you to collaborate with them on an ekphrastic art-to-poetry project. Think of questions that you would like to ask the artist about their work of art. Jot down your responses to one or more of these writing prompts, then convert the text into an iconographic ekphrastic poem. Reflect on how this exercise changes your poetic voice.
4. Jeff Davis (2008) recommended that writers practice yoga poetry on a daily basis. Yoga poetry is a writing practice that employs yoga to quiet the mind, increase focus, and activate emotional imagery and creativity. Davis argued that yoga is a muse for creative writing: By incorporating yogic awareness into our writing practice, we can enhance the mind–body connection and boost our capacity for writing embodied poetry. For the next 30 days, join a weekly yoga class and make a daily commitment to practicing yoga postures synchronized with your breathing. How does this practice change your poetic voice?
5. Readers who identify as yoga practitioners may want to try this exercise: The poem "Salute to the Sun," found in Table 3.1, is a yoga poem that I wrote. Each line of the poem corresponds to a posture in the sequence known as Surya Namaskar or the Sun Salutation. There are many different variations of this sequence. (See

Table 3.1 Yoga poetry exercise: salute to the sun

Posture	Breath	Line
Mountain	Exhale	The breath of the sun moves me
Arms extended mountain	Inhale	Like a kiss to the nape of my neck,
Forward bend	Exhale	It fills me with warmth
Half forward bend	Inhale	Near bursting with joy,
Half-plank	Exhale	I breathe, cool and deep
Upward dog	Inhale	The air in my shade and move on,
Downward dog	Exhale	Changing, but never ceasing
Half forward bend	Inhale	To become what I was
Forward bend	Exhale	And will be
Arms extended mountain	Inhale	Like a wave of desert sand,
Mountain	Exhale	The sun moves me

Ezrin, 2022, for some common permutations.) I used Sun Salutation A here, as its 11 steps are synchronized with the rhythm of my yoga poem, but you can practice your own version, as long as the number of steps match the number of lines in the poem. Before you begin, place a copy of the poem in a place where it is easy to see from your yoga mat. (I like to tape mine on the wall in front of me.) If you have limited vision, you could create an audio recording of the poem instead.

Stand in mountain pose and take a deep breath. On the exhalation, read the first line of the poem. Inhale, extending your arms overhead as you read the second line of the poem. Continue, moving through all of the postures in the sequence in tandem with each line of the poem. Feel free to experiment, adapting the postures, line breaks, and breathing until it feels right to you. Alternatively, write your own yoga poem to accompany your favorite sequence of yoga postures. Reflect on how this exercise affects your yoga practice, as well as your poetic voice.

References

Apol, L. (2021). *Poetry, poetic inquiry and Rwanda: Engaging with the lives of others*. Springer.
Barnell, C., & Barnell, A. (2016). *Grounds for a miracle* [Painting].
Butler-Kisber, L. (2010). *Qualitative inquiry: Thematic, narrative and arts-informed perspectives*. Sage.
Cameron, J. (1992). *The artist's way: A spiritual path to higher creativity*. G P. Putnam's Sons.
Coons, G. (2017). *Four ravens* [Painting]. https://gordoncoons.com/works/2361850/four-ravens
Davis, J. (2008). *The journey from the center to the page: Yoga philosophies and practices as muse for authentic writing*. Monkfish Book Publishing Co.
de Souza, R. (2019.) Working the hyphen from below: The "thick decryption of subtext" and the micro-politics of knowledge production. *Frontiers in Communication, 4,* (68), 1–12. https://doi.org/10.3389/fcomm.2019.00068

References

DeVinney, J. (2008a). *Interview with Patria Smith*. [Interview]. Traditional Arts Indiana Archive.

DeVinney, J. (2008b). *Interview with Katrina Mitten*. [Interview]. Traditional Arts Indiana Archive.

Ezrin, S. (2022, February 24). *A comprehensive guide to sun salutation sequences A, B, and C*. Healthline. https://www.healthline.com/health/fitness/sun-salutation-sequence

Faulkner, S., & Ruby, P. (2015). Feminist identity in romantic relationships: A relational dialectics analysis of email discourse as collaborative found poetry. *Women's Studies in Communication, 38*(2), 206–226. https://www.tandfonline.com/doi/full/10.1080/07491409.2015.1025460

Finlay, L. (2002). "Outing" the Researcher: The Provenance, Process, and Practice of Reflexivity. *Qualitative Health Research, 12*(4), 531. https://doi.org/10.1177/104973202129120052

Gomringer, E. (1968). *The book of hours and constellations*. Something Else Press, Inc.

Gouzouasis, P. (in press). Autoethnography: A reflexive research process. In P. Gouzouasis & C. Wiley (Eds.), *The companion of music, autoethnography, and reflexivity*. Routledge.

Gray, F. (2016). Little Turtle descendant keeps beadworking alive. *The Journal-Gazette (Fort Wayne, Indiana)*.

Gulla, A. N. (2018). Ekphrastic conversations: Writing poems as dialogues with works of art. *Canadian Review of Art Education: Research & Issues, 45*(1), 23–31.

James, K. (2009). Cut-up consciousness and talking trash: Poetic inquiry and the spambot's text. In M. Prendergast, C. Leggo, & P. Sameshima (Eds.), *Poetic inquiry: Vibrant voices in the social sciences* (pp. 59–74). Sense Publishers.

Jocks, C. R. (1996). Spirituality for sale: Sacred knowledge in the consumer age. *American Indian Quarterly, 20*(3/4), 415–431. https://doi.org/10.2307/1185785

Lahman, M. (2019). Email with the dead. *Qualitative Inquiry, 25*(9–10), 831–832. https://doi.org/10.1177/1077800418784324

Lahman, M., & DeOliveira, B. (2021). Poetry spheres, flower poems: A dimensional poetry experience. *Qualitative Inquiry, 27*(5), 622–625. https://doi.org/10.1177/1077800420941050

Lahman, M., & Richard, V. M. (2014). Appropriated poetry: Archival poetry in research. *Qualitative Inquiry, 20*(3), 344–355. https://doi.org/10.1177/1077800413489272

Lahman, M., Teman, E., & Richard, V. (2019). IRB as poetry. *Qualitative Inquiry, 25*(2), 200–214. https://doi.org/10.1177/10778004177445

Leavy, P. (2020). *Method meets art: Arts-based research practice* (3rd ed.). Guilford Press.

Meyer, M. (2017). Concrete research poetry: A visual representation of metaphor. *Art/Research International: A Transdisciplinary Journal, 2(1)*, 32–57. https://doi.org/10.18432/R2KS6F

Meyer, M. (2023). Retracing "The Gourd Dancers." In N. Honein & M. Mckeon (Eds.), *Land, language, and belonging: Poetic inquiries* (pp. 105–112). Vernon Press.

Miller, E. (2019). Creating research poetry: A nursing home example. In A. Humble & M. Radina (Eds.), *How qualitative data analysis happens: Moving beyond 'themes emerged'* (pp. 18–33). Routledge.

Olmos-Vega, F. M., Stalmeijer, R. E., Varpio, L., & Kahlke, R. (2023). A practical guide to reflexivity in qualitative research: AMEE Guide No. 149. *Medical Teacher, 45*(3), 241–251. https://doi.org/10.1080/0142159X.2022.2057287

Pappne Demecs, I., & Miller, E. (2019) Woven narratives: A craft encounter with tapestry weaving in a residential aged care facility. *Art/Research International: A Transdisciplinary Journal, 4(9)*, 256–286. https://doi.org/10.18432/ari29399

Penwarden, S., & Schoone, A. (2021). The pull of words: Reliving a poetry symposium through found poetry. *Art/Research International: A Transdisciplinary Journal, 6*(2), 347–368. https://doi.org/10.18432/ari29572

Publication manual of the American Psychological Association (7th ed.). (2020). American Psychological Association.

Richardson, L. (2000). Writing: A method of inquiry. In N. Denzin & Y. Lincoln (Eds.), *Handbook of qualitative research* (2nd ed., pp. 923–943). Sage.

Richardson, P., & Walsh, S. (2018). Endless open heart: Collaborative poetry and image as contemplative and restorative practice. *Canadian Review of Art Education: Research & Issues, 45*(1).

Rogers, R. (2006). From cultural exchange to transculturation: A review and reconceptualization of cultural appropriation. *Communication Theory, 16*, 474–503. https://doi.org/10.1111/j.1468-2885.2006.00277.x

Rose, W. (1980). *Lost copper*. Malki Museum.

Ruiz Castro, M. (2021). Intersectional reflexivity: Using intersectional reflexivity as a means to strengthen critical autoethnography. In V. Stead, C. Elliott, & S. Mavin (Eds.), *Handbook of research methods on gender and management* (pp. 214–230). Edward Elgar Publishing Limited. https://doi.org/10.4337/9781788977937.00023

Sameshima, P., & Wiebe, S. (2018). Faith, hope & love: Postscript on interprofessional processes for innovating generation/Foi, espoir et amour: Postscript sur les processus interprofessionnels de génération novatrice. *The Canadian Review of Art Education, 45*(1), 129–152. https://doi.org/10.26443/crae.v45i1.61

Schoone, A. (2018). The found poem as a constellation. In P. Sameshima, A. Fidyk, K. James, & C. Leggo (Eds.), *Poetic inquiry: Enchantment of place* (pp. 271–280). Vernon Press.

Schoone, A. (2019). An ekphrastic review of Ilona Pappne Demecs and Evonne Miller's "Woven narratives: A craft encounter with tapestry weaving in a residential aged care facility." *Art/Research International: A Transdisciplinary Journal, 4(1)*, 429–432. https://journals.library.ualberta.ca/ari/index.php/ari/issue/view/1943/showToc

Schoone, A. (2020). *Constellations of alternative education tutors: A poetic inquiry*. Springer. https://www.springer.com/gp/book/9783030354947

Simon, G. (2013). Relational ethnography: Writing and reading in research relationships. *Forum Qualitative Sozialforschung/Forum: Qualitative Social Research, 14(1)*. https://doi.org/10.17169/fqs-14.1.1735

Sjollema, S., & Yuen, F. (2018). Poetic representation, reflexivity and the recursive turn. In P. Sameshima, A. Fidyk, K. James, & C. Leggo (Eds.), *Poetic inquiry: Enchantment of place* (pp. 59–68). Vernon Press.

Smith, S. (n.d.) *Walking meditation practice*. Contemplative Mind. https://www.contemplativemind.org/practices/tree/walking-meditation

Tracy, S. (2013). *Qualitative research methods: Collecting evidence, crafting analysis, communicating impact*. John Wiley & Sons, Ltd.

Tracy, S. (2020). *Qualitative research methods: Collecting evidence, crafting analysis, communicating impact* (2nd ed.). John Wiley & Sons, Ltd.

United Nations Educational, Scientific, and Cultural Organization. (1989). Recommendation on the safeguarding of traditional culture and folklore. https://atom.archives.unesco.org/recommendation-on-safeguarding-of-traditional-culture-and-folklore

Open Access This chapter is licensed under the terms of the Creative Commons Attribution 4.0 International License (http://creativecommons.org/licenses/by/4.0/), which permits use, sharing, adaptation, distribution and reproduction in any medium or format, as long as you give appropriate credit to the original author(s) and the source, provide a link to the Creative Commons license and indicate if changes were made.

The images or other third party material in this chapter are included in the chapter's Creative Commons license, unless indicated otherwise in a credit line to the material. If material is not included in the chapter's Creative Commons license and your intended use is not permitted by statutory regulation or exceeds the permitted use, you will need to obtain permission directly from the copyright holder.

Chapter 4
Iconographic Research Poetry in the Classroom

Abstract In this chapter, the author explores techniques for integrating iconographic research poetry in the classroom. She begins by providing an overview of arts-based research (ABR) pedagogy. Next, she describes pedagogical innovations that embrace research poetry. Finally, the author offers readers a toolkit that they can use to incorporate iconographic research poetry into their qualitative research courses. She contends that by introducing poetic inquiry into the research methods classroom, qualitative research instructors can cultivate creativity and encourage students to begin thinking about concepts like crystallization and alternative representation of findings.

Keywords Arts-based research (ABR) · Arts-based educational research (ABER) · ABR methods · ABR pedagogy · Crystallization · Iconographic research poetry · Research poetry

This chapter explores techniques for integrating iconographic research poetry in the classroom. I begin by providing an overview of arts-based research (ABR) pedagogy (Barone & Eisner, 2006; Bresler, 2018; Dixon & Senior, 2009). Next, I describe pedagogical innovations that embrace research poetry (e.g., Benton & Russell, 2016; Guyas & Keys, 2009; Jacob & Kincaid, 2018; Lahman & DeOliveira, 2021; Lapum & Hume, 2015; Leggo, 2005; Meyer & Helmer, in press; Romero, 2020). Finally, I offer readers a toolkit that they can use to incorporate iconographic research poetry into their qualitative research courses. In the toolkit, I adapt techniques developed by writers who teach (e.g., Addonizio, 2009; Cohen, 2009; Padgett, 2000) in an effort to generate poetry-centered exercises for the classroom. By prompting students to create a broadside (a poem incorporating an image), a shape poem with line breaks, or a found poem shaped like a calligram, qualitative research instructors can cultivate creativity in the research methods classroom and encourage students to begin thinking about concepts like crystallization and alternative representation of findings (Ellingson, 2009; Richardson, 2000).

© The Author(s) 2024
M. Meyer, *Iconographic Research Poetry*,
SpringerBriefs in Arts-Based Educational Research,
https://doi.org/10.1007/978-981-97-2375-1_4

4.1 Arts-Based Research Pedagogy

According to Bresler (2018), ABR pedagogy seeks to produce "expanded seeing, listening, and understanding of outer and inner landscapes through resonance with artworks in the role of a viewer or a maker" (p. 651). Teacher-scholars from a variety of disciplines, including communication studies, education, social work, sociology, and theater (e.g., Benton & Russell, 2016; Lapum & Hume, 2015; Leavy, 2009, 2015; Meyer & Helmer, in press; Norris, 2011; Romero, 2020) have embraced ABR practices such as writing poetry, creative nonfiction, and scripts; performing music, dance, and theatre; creating visual art and crafts; and producing documentaries. Dixon and Senior (2009) framed ABR instruction as "transgressive pedagogy" (p. 9), a creative alternative to traditional teaching methods. Recently, scholars (e.g., Benton & Russell, 2016; Lapum & Hume, 2015; Romero, 2020) have demonstrated that ABR methods increase student engagement and foster students' curiosity and creativity. Leggo (2005) argued that poetry, in particular, invites creativity and creative living, which in turn promote transformative learning. Jacob and Kincaid (2018) found that integrating poetry into the curriculum was associated with positive learning outcomes. Indeed, Traver (2018) reported that students who learned sociology through poetry felt encouraged to write, to read carefully, to think creatively, and to expand their vocabulary. Romero (2020) noted that students developed enhanced empathy and analytical skills, as well. In addition, Raingruber (2009) observed that poetry reading helped students develop an appreciation for ambiguity in language, a skill that is needed to conduct qualitative analysis.

A number of parallels can be drawn between arts-based research and arts-based pedagogy. First, both practices are question-oriented. In his poem, "essences of inspirational pedagogy," Schoone (2020) wrote

> what if?
>
> is not a method
>
> it's
>
> life

As Schoone aptly observed, arts-based pedagogy seeks to inspire students by asking them questions, rather than spoon-feeding them answers. Like arts-based educational research, arts-based pedagogy raises more questions than it answers (Barone & Eisner, 2006). Bresler (2018) noted that "(traditional) research courses tend to emphasize accumulation of knowledge and skills, silencing, even shaming *unknowing*, thus ignoring its role in propelling perception and engagement" (p. 653). In contrast, ABR methods promote student curiosity (Benton & Russell, 2016; Lapum & Hume, 2015) and appreciation for ambiguity (Raingruber, 2009).

Second, both arts-based research and arts-based pedagogy value process over product. Researchers and students are not expected to produce professional works of art—they are only asked to engage in the artistic process. In a related manner, ABR pedagogy invites students to work at a relaxed pace that allows them to practice their

Table 4.1 Benefits associated with teaching iconographic research poetry

Teaching iconographic research poetry can
1. Increase student engagement
2. Foster students' curiosity and creativity
3. Encourage students to write, to read carefully, and to expand their vocabulary
4. Build positive relationships between students and instructors
5. Contextualize course content
6. Encourage students to create arts-based representations of research projects
7. Be a fun way to teach qualitative research

craft and reflect on the ways in which they are affected by their practice. Bresler (2018) noted that this slower pace facilitates relationship building. Just as poetic inquiry is a way of being in the world as well as a research method (Prendergast, 2009), arts-based pedagogy is a way of building community in addition to a method of teaching. As Prior (2018) concluded, "Seeing art as a process, in which understanding is constructed and co-constructed with others, is very much at the heart of using art as research." (p. 11). Clearly, the processual and relational emphases of arts-based research extend to arts-based practices in teaching and learning.

Incorporating arts-based pedagogy in the classroom may have positive relational implications for students and instructors. Norris (2011) advocated implementing concrete poetry as an icebreaker activity in an introductory graduate course for in-service teachers. Guyas and Keys (2009) identified arts-based educational inquiry in dissertation research as a site for emerging mentorship. Bresler (2018) argued that "ABR pedagogies entail a different pace that is... dedicated to processing and incubation" (p. 657). ABR's processual focus may be conducive to developing meaningful relationships in a community of learners who support one another in their arts-based journeys. In a recent collaborative ethnographic study about the experiences of teaching and learning in an arts-based organizational culture class (Meyer & Helmer, in press), my colleague and I found that students developed positive collaborative relationships in which graduate students mentored undergraduate students, members pulled their own weight, and individuals appreciated the unique contributions that various group members made to the teams' ABR projects. (See Table 4.1.)

4.2 Pedagogical Innovations

Instructors have used a variety of techniques to incorporate ABR into the classroom. Some instructors use ABR as a method for contextualizing course content, whereas others use ABR as a means to encourage students to create arts-based representations of research projects. Still others have used concrete poetry as a mechanism for building relationships. For example, Norris (2011) asked graduate students to introduce themselves using concrete poetry, an activity designed to encourage students to think about themselves in nontraditional ways and to use an arts-based medium to communicate and process information.

Lapum and Hume (2015) employed ABR to contextualize course content by using poetry, film, dance, and story to teach graduate students about abstract qualitative research concepts. In one assignment, the instructor asked students to read poetry and prose from an online blog about living with cystic fibrosis, then conduct a thematic analysis of the material, which became the basis for a discussion about interpretive analysis.

Lahman and DeOliveira (2021) also incorporated research poetry into a graduate-level qualitative research course. The authors designed a class activity in which they asked graduate students to create three-dimensional found poems derived from handwritten or computer-printed lines of interview transcripts and researcher's reflections. Using brads, narrow strips of paper, fine tip markers, lollipop sticks, and pipe cleaners, they instructed students to begin by choosing phrases from a research transcript or reflection paper. Next, students wrote or typed the phrases in single lines, which they cut on strips of the same width and length. By punching holes on each end of the line, stacking the slips of paper, and securing the stack by inserting a brad in each end, students created three-dimensional poems in the shape of orbs. Lahman and DeOliveira gave students the option of creating an alternative form, a poetry flower, by pinching both brads together, securing them in the middle, and affixing them to a lollipop stick or pipe cleaner. Students could hold their finished products in their hands or display multiple artifacts together in a vase, which provided them with a metaphorical opportunity to "stop and smell the roses" during the research process.

Traver (2018) incorporated poetry into an introductory sociology course to contextualize concepts for her students. Traver described her writing prompt in the following way:

> In a lecture on social identity, students were asked to write a poem that began "I am . . . ." Although these poems were collected by the author, they were used to verify students' comprehension of the course material—not to evaluate their creative expression.

Similarly, in an attempt to create a low-stakes environment that would encourage students to be creative, Benton and Russell (2016) offered the following extra credit option in a graduate-level social work class:

> Individually, students will select the research project (social justice issue) that is addressed by the program you have evaluated in your program/practice evaluation project and craft a format to creatively deliver this message, issue, and/or information. This project must be your own original work completed for this class. Some suggestions are, but are not limited to: art, photography, video, poetry, narratives, music/audio, socio-drama/acting, etc.

Romero (2020) created an opportunity for undergraduate honors sociology students to learn how to conduct an iterative inductive analysis by practicing poetic transcription. She began by assigning different sets of poems that addressed social justice issues to groups of students. She instructed students to analyze the poems as if they were data, using grounded theory techniques to identify emergent themes in the poems. Next, she asked each group to use poetic transcription to create an artistic representation of their findings. Students employed free verse and blackout poetry to generate poems that challenged the status quo, demonstrating their ability to think critically about oppressive power structures in society, as well as dominant methodological paradigms.

My colleague and I (Meyer & Helmer, in press) employed ABR as a method to encourage graduate and undergraduate communication studies students to create arts-based representations of research projects. I asked students to create arts-based representations of ethnographic research project findings in this way:

> Create an original arts-based representation related to your analysis. Products may include (but are not limited to) poetry, narrative, fiction, creative nonfiction, script, screenplay, music, dance, photography, video, visual art, sculpture, collage, sewing, baking, etc. The goal of this activity is to create something artistic that represents your findings, not to achieve perfection or produce a professional product. Feel free to work alone or in collaboration with your research partners.

Given that half of the assignments described thus far were geared toward ABR in general, rather than poetry, in particular, I consulted books about teaching and writing poetry (e.g., Addonizio, 2009; Cohen, 2009; Padgett, 2000) in an effort to generate poetry-centered exercises for the classroom. I have adapted these poets' writing exercises to offer some suggestions for integrating iconographic research poetry into the classroom.

Addonizio (2009) generated the following activity to create word/art, or a broadside (a poem incorporating an image):

> Ask a visual artist to respond to lines of your poetry, or to an entire poem, with a drawing or painting, or photograph. Print them together as a broadside . . . . [Alternatively], illustrate a short poem by someone else. (p. 265)

Addonizio's activity would be an excellent choice to encourage collaboration between poets and visual artists, a practice that I recommended in Chaps. 2 and 3. If students write and illustrate poems that represent their research findings, then the collaborative visual poems that they produce would be iconographic research poems.

Cohen (2009) developed a writing exercise designed to "work the white space" or shape poems with lines. To this end, she presented an excerpt from Jane Hirshfield's poem, "Lake and Maple," in paragraph form without the author's line breaks. She challenged the reader to "Take this paragraph and shape it into lines. Don't worry about right or wrong. Try to feel what shape would best embody the emotion, language, and narrative of the poem" (pp. 110–111). Cohen's exercise would be a good way to illustrate that there are many different ways to use space to complement the text of a poem. If the initial paragraph of text were taken from an interview transcript and the final shape reflected the theme of the excerpt, then the resulting poem would be an iconographic research poem.

Padgett (2000) offered two exercises related to found poetry and calligrams. If you ask students to explore these two exercises sequentially, the end result would be an iconographic research poem. First,

> Have each [student] select a passage from a book, newspaper, or conversation, write it down as if it were a poem, give it a title (which they might also find) and read it aloud . . . You might ask [students] why some found poems work better than others. (p. 119)

Next,

> To write a calligram, you might first want to choose a shape that has a clear outline, such as a basketball or a window. Then fill in the shape with words and lines that come to you when you think about a particular basketball game or a particular window you look out of. Or you might want the words to be spoken by the basketball or the window. Remember, you can make the words any size, style, or color you want. (p. 151)

If the shape that a student selects represents the theme of the text (e.g., a basketball-shaped poem that represents a conversation about basketball), then the poem would be an iconographic research poem.

4.3 Debriefing

Many of the ABR exercises presented above have clear connections with the processes of qualitative analysis (Tracy, 2013, 2020), crystallization (Ellingson, 2009), and creative analytic practices (Richardson, 2000). Recall from Chap. 1 that crystallization involves the representation of research findings via multiple genres. Richardson (2000) generated 21 creative analytic writing practices that could be adapted for classroom use (pp. 941–943). Embedded in her writing exercises are questions that would be interesting to ask students as you debrief any of the assignments described above. For example, if you instruct students to create research poems out of interview transcripts, you might ask them, "What do you know about the interviewee and about yourself that you did not know before you wrote the poem?" and "What poetic devices have you sacrificed in the name of science?" Alternatively, if you instruct students to create multiple representations of their data (e.g., a poem, an image, and an iconographic poem), you might inquire, "What do you know in each rendition that you did not know in the other renditions?" and "How do the different renditions enrich each other?"

Romero (2020) and Meyer and Helmer (in press) prompted students to write self-reflection essays after they presented their arts-based research projects. Some of the questions that they asked may help students process their experiences verbally or in writing. Romero asked students to identify "the skills they built practicing poetic transcription, how they might use these skills later in life or other research, and how the assignment helped them become better sociologists" (p. 215). Similarly, I asked my students

> What did you learn about organizational culture and doing ethnographic research? Did you feel motivated to learn about these subjects? Why or why not? What did you learn about yourself? . . . your research partners? . . . your interviewee? Did your view of yourself as an artist or creative person change over the course of the semester? If so, how? How would you feel about volunteering in the future for the organization that you studied? (p. 4)

Queries such as these can guide students to reflect on the extent to which the ABR exercises helped them achieve desired learning outcomes. Instructors can also analyze students' essays to assess the effectiveness of ABR exercises and assignments in meeting course learning outcomes. Alternatively, they could create iconographic research poems from students' responses (e.g., the mountain poem in Fig. 2.1).

Whether you decide to incorporate iconographic research poetry into a semester-long research project, an in-class writing exercise, or both, I hope that the assignments and activities presented in this chapter will help you expand your arts-based repertoire in the classroom. By embracing ABR pedagogy as an alternative to traditional teaching methods, you will give your students and yourself an opportunity to cultivate curiosity and creativity in teaching and learning. Besides, what could possibly be a more fun way to teach qualitative research methods?

References

Addonizio, K. (2009). *Ordinary genius*. W. W. Norton & Company.
Barone, T., & Eisner, E. (2006). Arts-based educational research. In J. Green, G. Camilli, P. Elmore, A. Skukauskaite, & E. Grace (Eds.), *Handbook of complementary methods in education research* (pp. 95–110). Lawrence Erlbaum Associates.
Benton, A., & Russell, A. (2016). "Using the other side of my brain": Creativity in the research classroom. *Journal of Poetry Therapy, 29*(3), 147–159. https://doi.org/10.1080/08893675.2016.1200257
Bresler, L. (2018). Aesthetic-based research as pedagogy: The interplay of knowing and unknowing toward expanded seeing. In P. Leavy (Ed.), *Handbook of arts-based research* (pp. 649–672). Guilford Press.
Cohen, S. (2009). *Writing the life poetic: An invitation to read & write poetry*. Writer's Digest Books.
Dixon, M., & Senior, K. (2009). Traversing theory and transgressing academic discourses: Arts-based research in teacher education. *International Journal of Education & the Arts, 10*(24), 1–21. http://www.ijea.org/v10n24
Ellingson, L. (2009). *Engaging crystallization in qualitative research: An introduction*. Sage.
Guyas, A. S., & Keys, K. (2009). Arts-based educational research as a site for emerging pedagogy and developing mentorship. *Visual Arts Research, 35*(2), 24–39. https://www.jstor.org/stable/20715500
Jacob, F., & Kincaid, S. (2018). *Poetry across the curriculum: New methods of writing intensive pedagogy for US community college and undergraduate education*. Brill | Sense.
Lahman, M., & DeOliveira, B. (2021). Poetry spheres, flower poems: A dimensional poetry experience. *Qualitative Inquiry, 27*(5), 622–625. https://doi.org/10.1177/1077800420941050
Lapum, J., & Hume, S. (2015). Teaching qualitative research: Fostering student curiosity through an arts-informed pedagogy. *The Qualitative Report, 20*(8), 1221–1233. http://www.nova.edu/ssss/QR/QR20/8/lapum2.pdf
Leavy, P. (2009). *Method meets art: Arts-based research practice*. Guilford Press.
Leavy, P. (2015). *Method meets art: Arts-based research practice* (2nd ed.). Guilford Press.
Leavy, P. (2020). *Method meets art: Arts-based research practice* (3rd ed.). Guilford Press.
Leggo, C. (2005). The heart of pedagogy: On poetic knowing and living. *Teachers and Teaching: Theory and Practice, 11*(5), 439–455. https://doi.org/10.1080/13450600500238436
Meyer, M., & Helmer, K. (in press). From "I am not a creative person" to "maybe I am a little artistic": Experiential learning, collaborative research, and arts-informed pedagogy in the neoliberal

academy. In F. Fovet (Ed.) *Implementing transformative student-centered pedagogies in the neoliberal ccademy: Constraints and opportunities.* CSMFL Publications.

Norris, J. (2011). Towards the use of the 'Great Wheel' as a model in determining the quality and merit of arts-based projects (research and instruction). *International Journal of Education & the Arts, 12*(1.7), 1–24. http://www.ijea.org/

Padgett, R. (2000). *The straight line: Writings on poetry and poets.* The University of Michigan Press.

Prendergast, M. (2009). Poetic inquiry is ... 29 ways of looking at poetry as qualitative research. *Educational Insights, 13(3).* http://einsights.ogpr.educ.ubc.ca/v13n03/intro/prendergast.html

Prior, R. (2018). Introduction: Artist-educator-researcher. In R. Prior (Ed.), *Using art as research in learning and teaching: Multidisciplinary approaches across the arts* (pp. 1–12). Intellect.

Raingruber, B. (2009). Assigning poetry reading as a way of introducing students to qualitative data analysis. *Journal of Advanced Nursing, 65*(8), 1753–1761.

Richardson, L. (2000). Writing: A method of inquiry. In N. Denzin & Y. Lincoln (Eds.), *Handbook of qualitative research* (2nd ed., pp. 923–943). Sage.

Romero, R. (2020). Poetic transcription in the sociology classroom: Developing empathy, analytical skills, creativity, and engagement. *Teaching Sociology, 48*(3), 211–219. https://doi.org/10.1177/0092055X20923703

Schoone, A. (2020). *Constellations of alternative education tutors: A poetic inquiry.* Springer. https://www.springer.com/gp/book/9783030354947

Tracy, S. (2013). *Qualitative research methods: Collecting evidence, crafting analysis, communicating impact.* Wiley.

Tracy, S. (2020). *Qualitative research methods: Collecting evidence, crafting analysis, communicating impact* (2nd ed.). Wiley.

Traver, A. (2018). Contextualizing math and poetry in community college courses: Impacts and implications in introduction to sociology. In F. Jacob & S. Kincaid (Eds.), *Poetry across the curriculum* (pp. 161–173). Brill | Sense.

Open Access This chapter is licensed under the terms of the Creative Commons Attribution 4.0 International License (http://creativecommons.org/licenses/by/4.0/), which permits use, sharing, adaptation, distribution and reproduction in any medium or format, as long as you give appropriate credit to the original author(s) and the source, provide a link to the Creative Commons license and indicate if changes were made.

The images or other third party material in this chapter are included in the chapter's Creative Commons license, unless indicated otherwise in a credit line to the material. If material is not included in the chapter's Creative Commons license and your intended use is not permitted by statutory regulation or exceeds the permitted use, you will need to obtain permission directly from the copyright holder.

Chapter 5
Conclusion and New Beginnings

Abstract In this chapter, the author offers a summary of the book, as well as a critical discussion about the strengths and limitations of iconographic research poetry. Next, she generates directions for future research, citing digital concrete poetic forms and installation art and poetry as inspiration for future experiments in iconographic research poetry. Finally, the author initiates a self-reflexive discussion about how she has been changed by this exercise in poetic inquiry—the process of writing a book about iconographic research poetry. She encourages readers to nurture the spirit of curiosity and playfulness that is inherent in us all by developing a regular writing practice, engaging in creative writing exercises, experimenting with poetic inquiry and iconographic research poetry in their scholarship, and integrating poetry-centered exercises in their teaching. The author concludes this chapter with a list of additional resources, including videos, digital archives, museum websites, and children's books that readers can consult to learn more about concrete and digital poetry, as well as poetic inquiry.

Keywords Arts-based research (ABR) · Arts-based educational research (ABER) · ABR methods · Concrete poetry · Digital poetry · Iconographic research poetry · Installation art · Living poetically · Poetic inquiry · Research poetry

This chapter offers a summary of the book, as well as a critical discussion about the strengths and limitations of iconographic research poetry and the implications of employing various media to represent one's research findings. I generate directions for future research, citing digital concrete poetic forms (e.g., Caselli, 2009) and installation art and poetry (e.g., Lapum, 2018; Lapum et al., 2014) as inspiration for future experiments in iconographic research poetry. I begin a self-reflexive discussion about how this exercise in poetic inquiry—the process of writing a book about iconographic research poetry—has changed me. As I continue this discussion in the postscript, I review literature about poetic inquiry ((Leggo, 2008; Prendergast 2009; Sameshima et al., 2018;) and identity (Clarke, 2014; Sjollema & Yuen, 2018) to explore how the practice of poetic inquiry can be a constant source of discovery and renewal for teacher-scholars. Toward this end, I encourage readers to nurture the spirit of curiosity and playfulness that is inherent in us all by developing a regular writing practice, engaging in creative writing exercises, experimenting with poetic inquiry and iconographic research poetry in their scholarship, and integrating poetry-centered exercises in their teaching. This chapter concludes with a list of additional resources, including videos, digital archives, museum websites, and children's books that readers can consult to learn more about concrete and digital poetry, as well as poetic inquiry.

5.1 Summary

The central goal of this book was to introduce readers to the craft of writing iconographic research poetry. In Chap. 1, I proposed iconographic research poetry as a novel form of poetic inquiry that bridges the art-science divide by melding aspects of concrete poetry, iconographic poetry, poetic inquiry, and research poetry. I began by defining and offering examples of key concepts such as concrete poetry, iconographic poetry, poetic inquiry, research poetry, and iconographic research poetry. By tracing the historical foundations of concrete poetry, iconographic poetry, poetic inquiry, and research poetry, four central areas of inquiry that have inspired the notion of iconographic research poetry, I offered readers an appreciation for the intellectual roots that inform this unique methodological approach. In the process, I invited two previously unrelated areas of inquiry into dialogue with one another. Finally, I considered the advantages of iconographic research poetry as a methodological innovation that bridges the humanities and the social sciences.

In Chap. 2, I offered a detailed description of the methods that can be used to create and design iconographic research poetry. I began by situating iconographic research poetry on the qualitative continuum (Ellingson, 2009). Next, I offered an overview of iterative thematic analysis (Tracy, 2013, 2020) and metaphor analysis (Tracy et al., 2006), two qualitative analytic methods. Drawing from the extant literature in research poetry and poetic inquiry (e.g., Ellingson, 2011; Faulkner, 2009, 2020; Glesne, 1997; Prendergast, 2012), concrete, iconographic, and visual poetry (e.g., Bohn, 2011; Kostelanetz, 1970; Solt, 1968; Swenson, 1970), and concrete and iconographic research poetry (Meyer, 2017; Miller, 2019; Schoone, 2018), I explicated the processes by which data can be represented in the form of iconographic research poetry. Next, I provided a step-by-step description of strategies that researchers can use to create iconographic research poetry from qualitative data. I described my methods of creating iconographic research poems with word processing software and graphic design programs using typed text, clip art or icons, and layered text and images. I discussed the importance of soliciting member reflections from participants and artist-poets. At the end of the chapter, I offered writing exercises designed to help aspiring iconographic research poets exercise their poetic imagination. Specifically, I asked readers to re-analyze an existing qualitative data set with the methods I previously described. By conducting a metaphor analysis, selecting a visual image to represent the metaphor, and creating an iconographic research poem with word processing software, I invited qualitative researchers to make their first foray into iconographic research poetry.

Chapter 3 provided a review of concrete and iconographic research poetry. I traced the development of concrete and iconographic research poetry in recent journal articles, book chapters, and books (e.g., Lahman & DeOliveira, 2021; Lahman et al., 2019; Meyer, 2017; Miller, 2019; Penwarden & Schoone, 2021; Schoone, 2018, 2019, 2020). In addition to describing and interpreting recently published exemplars, I shared some previously unpublished iconographic ekphrastic research poetry (e.g., "Grounds for a Miracle Backstory") that has promising implications for collaborative arts-based inquiry. Following my review, I engaged in a reflexive examination of ethical tensions that I experienced as a non-Native scholar writing about Native artists and their works of art. At the end of the chapter, I offered exercises designed to help writers develop their poetic inquiry practice. Specifically, I elaborated on techniques suggested by creative writing coaches (e.g., Cameron, 1992; Davis, 2008) and meditation teachers (e.g., Smith, n.d.), who instruct writers to enhance their creativity by writing morning pages, going on artist dates, practicing yoga poetry, and engaging in walking meditation.

Chapter 4 explored techniques for integrating iconographic research poetry in the classroom. I began by providing an overview of arts-based research pedagogy (Barone & Eisner, 2006; Bresler, 2018; Dixon & Senior, 2009). Next, I described pedagogical innovations that embrace research poetry (e.g., Benton & Russell, 2016; Guyas & Keys, 2009; Jacob & Kincaid, 2018; Lahman & DeOliveira, 2021; Lapum & Hume, 2015; Meyer & Helmer, in press; Romero, 2020). Finally, I offered readers a toolkit that they can use to incorporate iconographic research poetry into their qualitative research courses. In the toolkit, I adapted techniques developed by writers who teach (e.g., Addonizio, 2009; Cohen, 2009; Padgett, 2000) in an effort to generate poetry-centered exercises for the classroom. I suggested that qualitative research instructors could cultivate creativity in the research methods classroom by prompting students to create a broadside (a poem incorporating an image), a shape poem with line breaks, or a found poem shaped like a calligram. By encouraging students to begin thinking about concepts like crystallization and alternative representation of findings (Ellingson, 2009; Richardson, 2000) during exercise debriefing, instructors can link creative analytic practices with core qualitative research concepts.

5.2 Strengths and Limitations

In Chap. 1, I argued that there are a number of benefits to using iconographic poetic structures in research poetry. First, iconographic research poems provide greater insight than traditional qualitative analysis because they transform data into art. Second, iconographic poetry is a powerful device for representing metaphors because word-images convey metaphoric structure through visual cues. Third, iconographic poetry may be more easily understood than traditional research findings and conventional forms of poetry because it enlists visual images to help shape the reader's interpretation. This characteristic can enable scholars to translate their research into a more accessible format that can be appreciated by both academics and community members. As a form of poetic inquiry, it can also be a catalyst for inviting creativity into teacher-scholar-students' daily lives. For these reasons, I believe iconographic research poetry is a promising methodological innovation for arts-based researchers who are interested in issues such as crystallization, metaphor, representation, and disseminating their findings to the public.

In response to my enthusiastic endorsement of iconographic research poetry, some social scientists may argue that iconographic research poetry does not significantly improve upon either traditional qualitative research reports or existing forms of research poetry. In addition, some literary scholars may critique iconographic research poetry because it is not as elegantly crafted as the existing corpus of found, concrete, or iconographic poetry. Moreover, some artists may have disdain for iconographic research poetry because it is not as aesthetically pleasing as images created by visual artists. Finally, there may be digital technology whizzes who object to the use of static, two-dimensional Microsoft clip art- and icon-enabled images as forms of representation. Indeed, this is the classic double-bind that arts-based researchers face: Artists do not find ABR to be artistic enough and scientists do not find ABR to be scientific enough.

In Chap. 1, I acknowledged the ongoing conversation about criteria for evaluating research poetry (Faulkner, 2007, 2009, 2020; Lahman & Richard, 2014; Lahman et al., 2011; Percer, 2002; Richardson, 2000). This conversation is part of a broader discussion about evaluation criteria in arts-based research (Barone & Eisner, 2006; Chilton & Leavy, 2014; Leavy, 2009, 2015, 2020; Norris, 2011). I appreciate Norris's (2011) Great Wheel, which identified pedagogy, poiesis, politics, and public positioning as compass points that each artist-scholar can use to situate and assess a project based on its intended purpose, because it invites the artist-scholar to think explicitly about what the goal of their project is and where it falls on the art-research spectrum. Similarly, I applaud Faulkner's (2009, 2020) Venn diagram that offered a visual representation of the overlap between criteria derived from science and art because it implies that it might be appropriate to evaluate some projects with more scientific criteria and others with more artistic criteria. If, for example, one views poetic inquiry in its broadest sense as "a way to be and become in the world" (Leggo, as cited in Sameshima et al., 2018, p. 16), then it stands to reason that it should merit different evaluation criteria than a research poem that was designed to represent research findings. However, when Faulkner expanded her focus from research poetry in 2009 to poetic inquiry in 2020, she did not address this issue explicitly or adapt her existing evaluation criteria. I suggest that Norris's (2011) criterion of pedagogy, which refers to the intellectual or emotional growth an artist experiences when they "come to understand the world differently as a result of blending the content to the unique artistic form" (p. 3) might be an alternative criterion that could be used to evaluate poetic inquiry.

Cognizant of the double-bind that arts-based researchers face, as well as the fact that evaluation criteria for poetic inquiry should be contextual, rather than universal, I would locate this iconographic research poetry project at the intersection of science, art, and pedagogy. Because my formal training is that of a social scientist and this book is intended to be a methods book, I am rooted more firmly in science than in art: I create research informed by art, rather than art informed by research. However, because I conduct poetic inquiry, as well as research poetry, and apply my method in the educational context, my branches are growing toward the pedagogical sector. As readers assess the strengths and limitations of this book, I urge them to weight scientific, poetic, artistic (Faulkner, 2020), and pedagogical (Norris (2011) evaluation criteria accordingly.

5.3 Directions for Future Research

In Chap. 1, I discussed digital poetry and installation art as relatively recent developments in the fields of concrete poetry and research poetry. The diverse, constantly evolving forms of digital poetry have exciting implications for future concrete and iconographic research poetry projects. As Spinelli (2007) observed, "poetry *is*—or at least is inseparable from—the means by which it is produced and distributed or transmitted" (p. 100). If "user-friendly" word processor art inhibits creativity (Farrar, 2016), then the use of new media should enable research poets to generate innovative forms of representation that are likely to capture the attention of twenty-first century readers. For example, kinetic, multimedia video poetry (e.g., Caselli, 2009) is a promising vehicle for research poets who seek to represent their subject in a unique way. The ability to juxtapose text, images and sound would allow scholars to communicate research findings in a manner that would engage viewers' eyes and ears. Alternatively, interactive poetry-art installations can create experiential encounters that evoke embodied emotions, challenge taken-for-granted assumptions, prompt critical reflection, and invite dialogue between researchers and audience members (Lapum, 2018; Lapum et al., 2014). Because of their immersive and interactive nature, poetry-art installations would be particularly powerful methods for engaging community members in public scholarship.

As I reflect on the myriad directions for future research that would be made possible by marrying research poetry with new media and installation art, I realize that the end of this book is also a beginning. Iconographic research poetry is an emergent arts-based research method that has the potential to spark conversations between social scientists, poets, artists, filmmakers, and digital media scholars. I hope that readers who experiment with the techniques described in this book will use their expertise to improve my proposed methodology and continue to expand the boundaries of what we know to be research poetry and poetic inquiry. I invite you to contact me if you would like to share your thoughts and feelings about this book. I look forward to the possibility of engaging in dialogue with you in order to further the advancement of iconographic research poetry as an arts-based research method.

5.4 Poetic Inquiry as a Transformational Practice

In the preface, I described how I made the journey from a newly minted PhD student trained in the positivist tradition to an associate professor who reinvented herself as a creative qualitative scholar and research poet. My latest foray into poetic inquiry—the process of writing this book—has given me an opportunity to share a new form of research poetry, iconographic research poetry, with others who are interested in alternative forms of representation. I believe that this process has made me a better teacher, scholar, and writer. In addition, as I will explain in the postscript, poetic inquiry has enabled me to understand what it means to live poetically in community.

As I immersed myself in the literature about concrete poetry, iconographic research poetry, research poetry, qualitative analysis, and poetic inquiry, I began to appreciate iconographic research poetry as a creative form of inquiry that bridges the humanities, social science, and arts-based research. This transdisciplinary context allowed me to understand and explicate my approach to creating iconographic research poetry in a new way—not only as a creative process that I had employed in my own research, but also as a scientific and arts-based research method that I could teach to others. In sharing my passion for poetry with others, I initiated a dialogue in my local and global communities about the power of concrete and iconographic research poetry—and also the empowering aspect of transforming ourselves by reinventing what we do and how we do it. I vowed never again to lock my creativity away in a time capsule.

I hope that you will consider iconographic research poetry as a starting point for the next leg of your lifelong journey as a teacher-scholar-student. My experience leads me to believe that iconographic research poetry can be a powerful catalyst for reinventing who you are, what you do, and how you do it. After having read this book, I hope that you will feel motivated to produce your own creative work, as well as to share what you have learned with others. I envision that you or one of your students will adapt the methods in this book, thereby advancing iconographic research poetry as an arts-based research and pedagogical method.

5.5 Additional Resources

In addition to the scholarly sources cited in the writing exercises at the end of each chapter, I encourage you to consult the following scholarly books, journal articles, videos, websites, and children's books to learn more about concrete and digital poetry, as well as poetic inquiry:

American Educational Research Association. (n.d.) *Arts-Based Ed Research (ABER) Special Interest Group.* https://abersigaera.weebly.com/

Getty Museum. (2013, April 10). *How to make a visual poem.* [Video file]. Retrieved from https://www.youtube.com/watch?v=wWpMB6gmBYA

5.5 Additional Resources

Getty Research Institute. (n.d.) *Concrete poetry: Words and sounds in graphic space*. Retrieved on 7 February 2019 from https://www.getty.edu/research/exhibitions_events/exhibitions/concrete_poetry/

Getty Research Institute. (May 25, 2017). *"Paper pear paper": Charting the course of concrete poetry*. [Video file]. Retrieved from https://www.youtube.com/watch?v=Ncduah3RNXg

International Congress on Qualitative Inquiry (n.d.). *SIG in Arts-Based Research*. https://icqi.org/sig-in-arts-based-research/

International Symposium on Poetic Inquiry (n.d.) https://www.poeticinquiry.ca/

Janeczko, P., & Raschka, C. (2005). *A poke in the I : A selection of concrete poems*. Candlewick Press.

Kapell, D., & Steenland, S. (1998). *Kids' magnetic poetry book and creativity kit*. Workman Publishing.

McGill University. (n.d.) *Artful Inquiry Research Group (AIRG)*. https://www.mcgill.ca/artful-inquiry/airg

Moving Poems (n.d.) *The best poetry videos on the web*. https://movingpoems.com/

Poem Generator. (n.d.) *Create a concrete poem*. Retrieved on 7 February 2019 from https://www.poem-generator.org.uk/concrete/

Sackner Archive of Concrete and Visual Poetry. (n.d.) *The Sackner archive of concrete and visual poetry*. Retrieved on 7 February 2019 from http://ww3.rediscov.com/sacknerarchives/Welcome.aspx

Sark (1993). *Sark's journal and play!book: A place to dream while awake*. Celestial Arts.

TED-Ed. (n.d.) *There's a poem for that*. https://www.youtube.com/playlist?list=PLJicmE8fK0Egxi0hgy5Tw-NFyLcpJ4bzJ

Ubuweb. (n.d.). *UbuWeb: All avant-garde*. http://www.ubu.com/

University of Pennsylvania. (n.d.). *Electronic Poetry Center*. https://writing.upenn.edu/epc/

University of Pittsburg. (2019). *Latin American concrete poetry and artists' books: Additional resources*. https://pitt.libguides.com/latinamericanconcretepoetry/additionalresources

Vispo. (n.d.) Vispo~Langu(im)age: Experimental visual poetry, literary programming, and essays on new media by Jim Andrews. https://vispo.com/index2.html

As the children's books and Sark's journal illustrate, concrete poetry is an inherently playful practice. At the same time that you integrate concrete and iconographic research poetry into your life as a teacher-scholar-student, make sure that you also cultivate your sense of playfulness: Remember that "play is fun, first of all, a concept that often gets lost as we work in academia" (Ellingson, 2009, p. 81). Toward that end, remain open-minded and open-hearted. Don't take yourself too seriously. Give yourself permission to play. Be creative!

References

Addonizio, K. (2009). *Ordinary genius*. W. W. Norton & Company.
Barone, T., & Eisner, E. (2006). Arts-based educational research. In J. Green, G. Camilli, P. Elmore, A. Skukauskaite, & E. Grace (Eds.), *Handbook of complementary methods in education research* (pp. 95–110). Lawrence Erlbaum Associates.
Benton, A., & Russell, A. (2016). "Using the other side of my brain": Creativity in the research classroom. *Journal of Poetry Therapy, 29*(3), 147–159. https://doi.org/10.1080/08893675.2016.1200257
Bohn, W. (2011). *Reading visual poetry*. Fairleigh Dickinson University Press.
Bresler, L. (2018). Aesthetic-based research as pedagogy: The interplay of knowing and unknowing toward expanded seeing. In P. Leavy (Ed.), *Handbook of arts-based research* (pp. 649–672). Guilford Press.
Cameron, J. (1992). *The artist's way: A spiritual path to higher creativity*. G P. Putnam's Sons.
Caselli, C. (2009, 23 June). *Cinco poemas concretos*. [Video poem]. Moving Poems. https://movingpoems.com/2009/06/cinco-poemas-concretos-five-concrete-poems/
Chilton, G., & Leavy, P. (2014). Arts-based research practice: Merging social research and the creative arts. In P. Leavy (Ed.), The Oxford handbook of qualitative research (pp. 403–422.) Oxford University Press.
Clarke, C. (2014). Liminal lives: Navigating the spaces between (poet and scholar). *In Education, 20*(2), 103–120.
Cohen, S. (2009). *Writing the life poetic: An invitation to read & write poetry*. Writer's Digest Books.
Davis, J. (2008). *The journey from the center to the page: Yoga philosophies and practices as muse for authentic writing*. Monkfish Book Publishing Co.
Dixon, M., & Senior, K. (2009). Traversing theory and transgressing academic discourses: Arts-based research in teacher education. *International Journal of Education & the Arts, 10*(24), 1–21. http://www.ijea.org/v10n24
Ellingson, L. (2009). *Engaging crystallization in qualitative research: An introduction*. Sage.
Ellingson, L. (2011). The poetics of professionalism among dialysis technicians. *Health Communication, 26*(1), 1–12. https://doi.org/10.1080/10410236.2011.527617
Farrar, R. (2016). Word processor art: How "user-friendly" inhibits creativity. *Digital Humanities Quarterly, 10*(1).
Faulkner, S. (2007). Concern with craft: Using Ars Poetica as criteria for reading research poetry. *Qualitative Inquiry, 13*(2), 218–234. https://doi.org/10.1177/1077800406295636
Faulkner, S. (2009). *Poetry as method: Reporting research through verse*. Left Coast Press.
Faulkner, S. (2020). *Poetic inquiry: Craft, method, and practice* (2nd ed.). Routledge.
Guyas, A. S., & Keys, K. (2009). Arts-based educational research as a site for emerging pedagogy and developing mentorship. *Visual Arts Research, 35*(2), 24–39. https://www.jstor.org/stable/20715500
Jacob, F., & Kincaid, S. (2018). *Poetry across the curriculum: New methods of writing intensive pedagogy for US community college and undergraduate education*. Brill | Sense.
Kostelanetz, R. (1970). *Imaged words & worded images*. Outerbridge & Dienstfrey.
Lahman, M., & DeOliveira, B. (2021). Poetry spheres, flower poems: A dimensional poetry experience. *Qualitative Inquiry, 27*(5), 622–625. https://doi.org/10.1177/1077800420941050
Lahman, M., Rodriguez, K., Richard, V., Geist, M., Schende, R., & Graglia, P. (2011). (Re)forming research poetry. *Qualitative Inquiry*, 17(9), 887-896. https://doi.org/10.1177/1077800411423219
Lahman, M., & Richard, V. M. (2014). Appropriated poetry: Archival poetry in research. *Qualitative Inquiry, 20*(3), 344–355. https://doi.org/10.1177/1077800413489272
Lahman, M., Teman, E., & Richard, V. (2019). IRB as poetry. *Qualitative Inquiry, 25*(2), 200–214. https://doi.org/10.1177/1077800417774455

References

Lapum, J. (2018). Installation art: The voyage never ends. In P. Leavy (Ed.), *Handbook of arts-based research* (pp. 377–395). Guilford Press.

Lapum, J., & Hume, S. (2015). Teaching qualitative research: Fostering student curiosity through an arts-informed pedagogy. *The Qualitative Report, 20*(8), 1221–1233. http://www.nova.edu/ssss/QR/QR20/8/lapum2.pdf

Lapum, J. L., Liu, L., Church, K., Yau, T. M., Ruttonsha, P., Matthews David, A., & Retta, B. (2014). Arts-informed research dissemination in the health sciences: An evaluation of peoples' responses to "The 7,024th Patient" art installation. *SAGE Open, 4*(1), 2158244014524211.

Leavy, P. (2009). *Method meets art: Arts-based research practice*. Guilford Press.

Leavy, P. (2015). *Method meets art: Arts-based research practice*. (2nd ed.). Guilford Press.

Leavy, P. (2020). *Method meets art: Arts-based research practice*. (3rd ed.). Guilford Press.

Leggo, C. (2008). Astonishing silence: Knowing in poetry. In J.G. Knowles, & A. L. Cole, A. L. (Eds.), *Handbook of the Arts in Qualitative Research* (pp. 165–174). Sage.

Meyer, M. (2017). Concrete research poetry: A visual representation of metaphor. *Art/Research International: A Transdisciplinary Journal, 2(1),* 32–57. https://doi.org/10.18432/R2KS6F

Meyer, M., & Helmer, K. (in press). From "I am not a creative person" to "maybe I am a little artistic": Experiential learning, collaborative research, and arts-informed pedagogy in the neoliberal academy. In F. Fovet (Ed.) *Implementing transformative student-centered pedagogies in the neoliberal academy: Constraints and pportunities.* CSMFL Publications.

Miller, E. (2019). Creating research poetry: A nursing home example. In A. Humble & M. Radina (Eds.), *How qualitative data analysis happens: Moving beyond 'themes emerged'* (pp. 18–33). Routledge.

Moving Poems (n.d.) *The best poetry videos on the web.* https://movingpoems.com/

Norris, J. (2011). Towards the use of the 'Great Wheel' as a model in determining the quality and merit of arts-based projects (research and instruction). *International Journal of Education & the Arts, 12 (1.7),* 1–24. http://www.ijea.org/

Padgett, R. (2000). *The straight line: Writings on poetry and poets.* The University of Michigan Press.

Penwarden, S., & Schoone, A. (2021). The pull of words: Reliving a poetry symposium through found poetry. *Art/Research International: A Transdisciplinary Journal, 6*(2), 347–368. https://doi.org/10.18432/ari29572

Percer, L. H. (2002). Going beyond the demonstrable range in educational scholarship: Exploring the intersections of poetry and research. *The Qualitative Report, 7*(2). http://www.nova.edu/ssss/QR/QR7-2/hayespercer.html

Poem Generator. (n.d.) https://www.poem-generator.org.uk/

Prendergast, M. (2009). Poetic inquiry is … 29 ways of looking at poetry as qualitative research. *Educational Insights, 13*(3). http://einsights.ogpr.educ.ubc.ca/v13n03/intro/prendergast.html

Prendergast, M. (2012). Education and/as art: A found poetry suite. *International Journal of Education & the Arts, 13*(2), 1–18.

Richardson, L. (2000). Writing: A method of inquiry. In N. Denzin & Y. Lincoln (Eds.), *Handbook of qualitative research* (2nd ed., pp. 923–943). Sage.

Romero, R. (2020). Poetic transcription in the sociology classroom: Developing empathy, analytical skills, creativity, and engagement. *Teaching Sociology, 48*(3), 211–219. https://doi.org/10.1177/0092055X20923703

Sameshima, P., Fidyk, A., James, K., & Leggo, C. (2018). *Poetic inquiry: Enchantment of place.* Vernon Press.

Sark (1993). *Sark's journal and play!book: A place to dream while awake.* Berkeley, CA: Celestial Arts.

Schoone, A. (2018). The found poem as a constellation. In P. Sameshima, A. Fidyk, K. James, & C. Leggo (Eds.), *Poetic inquiry: Enchantment of place* (pp. 271–280). Vernon Press.

Schoone, A. (2019). An ekphrastic review of Ilona Pappne Demecs and Evonne Miller's "Woven narratives: A craft encounter with tapestry weaving in a residential aged care facility." *Art/*

Research International: A Transdisciplinary Journal, 4(1), 429–432. https://journals.library.ualberta.ca/ari/index.php/ari/issue/view/1943/showToc

Schoone, A. (2020). *Constellations of alternative education tutors: A poetic inquiry.* Springer. https://www.springer.com/gp/book/9783030354947

Sjollema, S., & Yuen, F. (2018). Poetic representation, reflexivity and the recursive turn. In P. Sameshima, A. Fidyk, K. James, & C. Leggo (Eds.), *Poetic inquiry: Enchantment of place* (pp. 59–68). Vernon Press.

Smith, S. (n.d.). *Walking meditation practice.* Contemplative Mind. https://www.contemplativemind.org/practices/tree/walking-meditation

Solt, M. (1968). *Concrete poetry: A world view.* Indiana University Press.

Spinelli, M. (2007). Electric line: The poetics of digital audio editing. In A. Morris & T. Swiss (Eds.), *New media poetics: Contexts, technotexts, and theories* (pp. 99–122). The MIT Press.

Swenson, M. (1970). *Iconographs.* Charles Scribner's Sons.

TED-Ed. (n.d.) *There's a poem for that.* https://www.youtube.com/playlist?list=PLJicmE8fK0Egxi0hgy5Tw-NFyLcpJ4bzJ

The International Symposium on Poetic Inquiry (n.d.) https://www.poeticinquiry.ca/

Tracy, S. (2013). *Qualitative research methods: Collecting evidence, crafting analysis, communicating impact.* John Wiley & Sons, Ltd.

Tracy, S., Lutgen-Sandvik, P., & Alberts, J. (2006). Nightmares, demons, and slaves: Exploring the painful metaphors of workplace bullying. *Management Communication Quarterly, 20*(2), 148–185. https://doi.org/10.1177/0893318906291980

Tracy, S. (2020). *Qualitative research methods: Collecting evidence, crafting analysis, communicating impact.* (2nd ed.). John Wiley & Sons, Ltd.

Ubuweb. (n.d.). *UbuWeb: All avant-garde.* http://www.ubu.com/

University of Pennsylvania. (n.d.). *Electronic Poetry Center.* https://writing.upenn.edu/epc/

University of Pittsburg Library System. (2022). *Latin American concrete poetry and artists' books: Additional resources.* https://pitt.libguides.com/latinamericanconcretepoetry

Vispo. (n.d.). *Vispo~Langu(im)age: Experimental visual poetry, literary programming, and essays on new media by Jim Andrews.* https://vispo.com/index2.html

Open Access This chapter is licensed under the terms of the Creative Commons Attribution 4.0 International License (http://creativecommons.org/licenses/by/4.0/), which permits use, sharing, adaptation, distribution and reproduction in any medium or format, as long as you give appropriate credit to the original author(s) and the source, provide a link to the Creative Commons license and indicate if changes were made.

The images or other third party material in this chapter are included in the chapter's Creative Commons license, unless indicated otherwise in a credit line to the material. If material is not included in the chapter's Creative Commons license and your intended use is not permitted by statutory regulation or exceeds the permitted use, you will need to obtain permission directly from the copyright holder.

Chapter 6
Postscript

Abstract In this postscript, the author explores what it means for her to live poetically in community. She begins by describing how she felt discouraged writing this book during the pandemic. Next, she explains how she coped with the unexpected loss of her best friend by writing poetry and creating a "constellation of memories," a 3-dimensional arboreal mobile of words and images, as part of a musical celebration of his life. She discusses how these practices helped her process the emotions of a difficult loss and brought a community of people together to celebrate the life of a loved one. By reviewing literature about poetic inquiry and identity, the author considers how the practice of poetic inquiry can be a constant source of consolation, discovery, and renewal for teacher-scholars, as well as the members of the local–global communities in which we live and write.

Keywords Community · Constellation of memories · Loss · Identity · Living poetically · Poetic inquiry

There were times during the process of writing this book that I felt discouraged. I was fortunate to be granted a sabbatical during which I completed my proposal and the first draft of this book. I felt quite privileged to be able to focus full-time on my research and writing. When I returned to teaching, I found it difficult to find the time (and also the peace and quiet, in a department full of extroverts) to move the project forward. Although I love teaching, I looked forward to the following summer, when I would be able to devote myself exclusively to working on revising my first draft. And then the pandemic changed everything.

Anyone who teaches knows that 2020 was an exceptionally challenging year because we had to pivot to remote learning mid-year. Most of us had only minimal training in online teaching and learning. I had never taught online before, so I spent a great deal of time and energy learning to teach remotely at the same time that I was teaching my classes. I was exhausted just trying to keep my head above water. My hands ached and my eyes squinted from working on a tiny laptop. Needless to say, this book project was shelved. I told myself that I would get back to it as soon as the semester was over. Unfortunately, when I requested access to my office, where my materials and equipment for writing the book were located, I was told that my research was "nonessential" by an administrator (who had not earned a PhD and did not conduct research). I felt simultaneously livid and demoralized.

During this time, I tried to remain positive and focus on the bright side: At least this summer I wouldn't have to work full-time without being paid! I took time to catch up on my pleasure reading and went for a bike ride every day. When it was safe to do so, I shared a meal and went for a walk in the woods with my best friend. I also enrolled in a boot camp for online instruction, so that I felt more prepared when fall semester rolled around and I was assigned to teach HyFlex classes (a hybrid of online and face-to-face instruction that offer flexibility in teaching during a pandemic).

And then one day my best friend, Stan, was diagnosed with stage 4 cancer. It was one of those situations when someone doesn't know they have cancer until they fracture their spine in multiple places. Because he decided not to seek treatment, we knew that he only had a short time to live. I spent as much time with him as I could over the next six weeks, sharing in-home hospice duties with his family and friends when I didn't have to be at work. I was physically and emotionally exhausted, but because we were not family members, I was not eligible for family leave. When he died, I was devastated. Working on my book was the furthest thing from my mind.

Some of Stan's friends and I decided to organize a musical celebration of his life. I wrote a poem for him, but I wasn't sure that I wanted to read it at the event because it did not have the celebratory tone that we were striving for. Still, I didn't want to leave it in the drawer. I wanted to share it with others who loved him and felt unraveled by his loss. (See Fig. 6.1.)

As I re-read the last line, "On that day, a constellation of starred memories will shine like fireflies in your mind's eye," it occurred to me that I could share my poem without having to read it aloud. I could embed it in a concrete representation of a constellation of memories of Stan. I remembered the concrete constellation poems that Schoone (2018, 2020) created in his poetic inquiry of alternative education tutors and Lapum et al.'s (2014) poetry and art installation. What if our community created an arboreal mobile of photos and written memories of Stan as a community art installation at the ceremony? We could print out small copies of our favorite photos of Stan, glue them on notecards and punch a hole on the top of the card. Then, we could affix glow-in-the-dark stars on the back of the card and tie the cards onto branches of a tree in the yard where we planned to hold the party.

At the base of the tree, we could place a small table with a pen and blank notecards that have punch holes at the top and glowing stars on the back. We could ask people to write down their favorite memory of Stan and hang it on the tree. While it's still light out, people could walk around and look at the pictures and read the memories. After dark, the stars would glow like a constellation of fireflies in the branches. We could take a series of photos of the arboreal mobile from day to dusk to night. After the party, we could take down the photos and cards, print out the constellation photos, and put them in a scrapbook for Stan's children to keep.

I felt so excited about this idea that I couldn't wait to share it with my friends who were co-hosting the celebration. One of them told me that it was a beautiful and perfect idea that would invite people to pause at the entrance of the party. A

6 Postscript

Fig. 6.1 Poem: "Unraveled"

In the time
when day meets night
and the sun and the moon
traverse the sky together,
you find that you are lost.

A delicate silver crescent
lights your way home.

You realize
life has become
a maze of black holes.
Abandonment.
Loss.
The one you love
Gone.

In the light of the moon
you recognize
how lucky
you have been.   fly.
You remember what it feels like   to
The electric buzz of good fortune
shimmers on your outstretched arms.

You know you have to mend,
to weave the night sky together
in a new direction, yet
when you try to stitch the clouds,
their noctilucent seams turn to mist.

Unraveled, you begin again.

It will take a season of tears
before the sun warms the earth
and the moon rejoins him in the sky.
On that day, a constellation of starred memories
will shine like fireflies in your mind's eye.

Fig. 6.2 Constellation of memories. [Photograph.] *Source* Michael Statler (2021). Used with permission

beautiful and perfect idea. A 3-dimensional concrete constellation of words and images inspired by Adrian Schoone and Jennifer Lapum, who saved my poem from the drawer. (See Fig. 6.2.)

6.1 Living Poetically in Community

The story that I shared about creating the constellation of memories exemplifies for me what it means to live poetically in community. Poetic inquiry is not only a method for creating alternative representations of research findings; it is also a way of being in the world (Prendergast, 2009). Akin to Leggo, I view the practice of writing poetry, "as a way of knowing and living, a way of examining lived experiences by attending to issues of identity, relationship, and community" (Leggo, 2008, p. 171). As I struggled to cope with the loss of my best friend, I processed my emotions by writing poetry. Unsure of whether or not I wanted to share my poem in a public setting, I meditated on the idea of "a constellation of memories." Recalling Schoone's (2018, 2020) concrete constellation poems and Lapum et al.'s (2014) poetry and art installation, I visualized an arboreal mobile of words and images, a community art installation and concrete representation of a constellation of memories of Stan. My friends responded to my idea with affirmation and support. Practicing poetic inquiry enabled me to travel from the precipice of a black hole of loss and loneliness to the warmth and light of a communal constellation of memories.

Leggo (2008) wrote "Poetry begins with attentiveness, imagination, mystery, enchantment. Poetry invites researchers to experiment with language, to create, to know, to engage creatively and imaginatively with experience" (p. 168). When life is replete with positive experiences, it doesn't take much effort to find the poetry in the beauty that surrounds us; however, when we face adversity, it can be difficult to find the frame of mind, as well as the time and energy, to be creative. It is precisely at these times we must be "vigilant about seeing the world with a poet's senses and heart and imagination" (James, 2018, p. 30). Indeed, the act of engaging in poetic inquiry can help us gain a different perspective on our situation. As Sjollema and Yuen (2018) observed, "poetic representation has much to teach about reflexivity, reflection: It emphasizes researcher intuition and emotion, having patience with the recursive process" (p. 66). Clearly, the process of writing autobiographical poetry shapes our identities as poets and scholars (Clarke, 2014). When we share our poetic inquiry with members of our community, we also change the fabric of our community. My experience with the constellation of memories leads me to believe that poetic inquiry can be a source of discovery and renewal not only for teacher-scholars, but also for the local–global communities in which we live and write.

References

Clarke, C. (2014). Liminal lives: Navigating the spaces between (poet and scholar). *In Education, 20*(2), 103–120.
James, K. (2018). What lovely words might also mean. In P. Sameshima, A. Fidyk, K. James, & C. Leggo (Eds.), *Poetic inquiry: Enchantment of place* (pp. 23–27). Vernon Press.
Lapum, J. L., Liu, L., Church, K., Yau, T. M., Ruttonsha, P., Matthews David, A., & Retta, B. (2014). Arts-informed research dissemination in the health sciences: An evaluation of peoples' responses to "The 7,024th Patient" art installation. *SAGE Open, 4*(1), 2158244014524211.
Leggo, C. (2008). Astonishing silence: Knowing in poetry. In J.G. Knowles, & A. L. Cole, A. L. (Eds.), *Handbook of the Arts in Qualitative Research* (pp. 165–174). Sage.
Prendergast, M. (2009). Poetic inquiry is ... 29 ways of looking at poetry as qualitative research. *Educational Insights, 13(3).* http://einsights.ogpr.educ.ubc.ca/v13n03/intro/prendergast.html
Schoone, A. (2018). The found poem as a constellation. In P. Sameshima, A. Fidyk, K. James, & C. Leggo (Eds.), *Poetic inquiry: Enchantment of place* (pp. 271–280). Vernon Press.
Schoone, A. (2020). *Constellations of alternative education tutors: A poetic inquiry.* Springer. https://www.springer.com/gp/book/9783030354947
Sjollema, S., & Yuen, F. (2018). Poetic representation, reflexivity and the recursive turn. In P. Sameshima, A. Fidyk, K. James, & C. Leggo (Eds.), *Poetic inquiry: Enchantment of place* (pp. 59–68). Vernon Press.
Statler, M. (2021). *Constellation of memories.* [Photograph].

Open Access This chapter is licensed under the terms of the Creative Commons Attribution 4.0 International License (http://creativecommons.org/licenses/by/4.0/), which permits use, sharing, adaptation, distribution and reproduction in any medium or format, as long as you give appropriate credit to the original author(s) and the source, provide a link to the Creative Commons license and indicate if changes were made.

The images or other third party material in this chapter are included in the chapter's Creative Commons license, unless indicated otherwise in a credit line to the material. If material is not included in the chapter's Creative Commons license and your intended use is not permitted by statutory regulation or exceeds the permitted use, you will need to obtain permission directly from the copyright holder.

Index

A
ABR, *see* arts-based research
Addonizio, K., 63
Analysis
　coding, 25–26
　metaphor, 25–26, 40
　thematic, 10, 25, 62
Arboreal mobile, 78, 80
Archival poetry, 47, 50–52
Arrière-garde, 9
Artist date, 55
Artist-poet reflections, 34, 48
Arts-based research
　pedagogical innovations, 61–64
　pedagogy, 60–61
Autobiographical poetry, 47, 81
Autoethnographic poetry, 5, 40, 45, 79
Avant-garde, 5

B
Barnell, A., 45–46
Barnell, C., 45–46
Barone, T., 60
Bean, V., 8
Benton, A., 60, 62
Bohn, W., 9, 29, 34
Bresler, L., 60–61
Butler-Kisber, L., 4, 10, 23, 45

C
Cameron, J., 55
Cannon, S., 13
Caselli, C., 9, 71
Charmaz, K., 25

Cluster poetry, 43
Cohen, S., 63
Collaborative
　ekphrasis, 45, 48, 63
　poetry, 48
Concrete poetry
　definition, 2
　exemplars, 2–4
　history, 5
Concrete research poetry, 1
　3-dimensional, 13, 41–42, 62
　exemplars, 42–44
Constellation of memories, 78, 80
Coons, G., 48, 50, 53
Creativity, 12, 14, 55, 60–61, 71
Crystallization, 14, 24, 64
Curiosity, 12, 60–61

D
DeOliveira, B., 42, 62
Digital poetic inquiry, 12–13
Digital poetry, 9, 71
Dixon, M., 60

E
Eisner, E., 60
Ekphrastic poetry, 41
Ellingson, L., 14, 24–25, 27, 73
Embodiment, 4, 27, 71
Ethics, 43, 53–54
Evaluation criteria
　poetic inquiry, 70
　research poetry, 12
Exercises

classroom, 61–64
debriefing, 64
iconographic research poetry, 35, 63–64
yoga poetry, 55–56

F
Faulkner, S., 4, 11, 27, 34, 47, 70
Found poetry, 4, 10–11, 28, 41–43, 50, 63
Free verse, 4, 62

G
Glesne, C., 10, 23, 28
Goldsmith, K., 9, 13
Gomringer, E., 7, 41
Gulla, A., 41, 54

H
Helmer, K., 61, 63–64
Hollander, J., 2, 5
Hume, S., 12, 60, 62

I
Iconographic ekphrastic poetic inquiry, 45, 47–52, 55
Iconographic poetry
    definition, 2
    exemplars, 8
    history, 5
Iconographic research poetry
    definition, 1, 5
    exemplars, 6, 29–35, 40
    future research, 71
    strengths and limitations, 14, 69
Indigenous languages, 5, 48
Installation art, 13, 71
International Symposium on Poetic Inquiry, 11, 43, 48
Interpretivism, 24

J
James, K., 13, 41, 81
Johnson, M., 26

K
Kostelanetz, R., 2, 7–8, 27

L
Lahman, M., 3–4, 12, 41–42, 44, 47, 50, 62

Lakoff, G., 26
Lapum, J., 12, 13, 60, 62, 71, 78, 80
Leavy, P., 4, 11, 24, 53
Leggo, C., 4, 10, 60, 70, 80–81
Lindlof, T., 25
Living poetically in community, 80
Loss, 78, 80

M
Malvini Redden, M., 26
McCabe, B., 8
Member reflections, 33–34
Metaphor, 8, 10, 26, 28, 31, 40
Methodology, 3, 24
    autoethnographic, 40, 45
    ethnographic, 40, 61
    narrative, 13, 42
    qualitative, 24, 53
Methods
    iconographic research poetry
        clip art/icons, 28–30, 35
        graphic design, 28, 30–33, 35
        typed text, 27–29, 35, 40, 42
Meyer, M., 5, 6, 14, 27, 34, 35, 40, 48, 51, 54, 61, 63, 64
Miller, E., 25, 28, 41, 44
Mindfulness, 55
Mitten, K., 50, 53
Morning pages, 55
Moving Poems, 9
Musical celebration of life, 78

N
Norris, J., 61, 70

O
Oliver, M., 26

P
Padgett, R., 63–64
Pandemic, 77–78
Paradigm, 24, 63
Penwarden, S., 43
Percer, L.H., 12
Perloff, M., 8
Poem Generator, 9
Poetic inquiry
    defining, 10, 12
    history, 9, 11
    iconographic, xi
    transformational practice, 72

Prendergast, M., 3, 11, 27, 61
Public research, 14

Q
Qualitative continuum, 24

R
Reflexivity, 52–54
   intersectional, 53
   relational, 53
Representation, 4, 8, 10, 14, 24, 27, 41, 45–47, 49, 51, 61–64, 71, 80
Research poetry
   defining, 4
   exemplars, 5
   history, 9
Resources, 72–73
Richardson, L., 9–10, 14, 52, 64
Romero, R., 62, 64

S
Sameshima, P., 4, 48
Schoone, A., 13, 28, 41–43, 60, 80
Sjollema, S., 4, 53, 81
Smith, P., 48–51, 53–54
Solt, M.E., 2, 4, 7, 28

Swenson, M., 2, 8, 27

T
Taylor, B., 25
Teaching qualitative research, 42, 61–63, 65
TED-Ed, 9
Tracy, S., 24–26, 33, 52
Traver, A., 60, 62
Typography, 27–29

U
UbuWeb, 9

V
Vispo, 9
Visual poetry, 9, 29

W
Walking meditation, 55
Williams, E., 7

Y
Yuen, F., 4–5, 53, 81

SPRINGER NATURE

GPSR Compliance

The European Union's (EU) General Product Safety Regulation (GPSR) is a set of rules that requires consumer products to be safe and our obligations to ensure this.

If you have any concerns about our products, you can contact us on ProductSafety@springernature.com

In case Publisher is established outside the EU, the EU authorized representative is:

Springer Nature Customer Service Center GmbH
Europaplatz 3
69115 Heidelberg, Germany

The manufacturer's authorised representative in the EU is Springer Nature Customer Service Centre GmbH, Europaplatz 3, 69115 Heidelberg, Germany. If you have any concerns regarding our products, please contact ProductSafety@springernature.com

Printed and bound by CPI Group (UK) Ltd, Croydon, CR0 4YY

23/03/2026

02076360-0008